collections

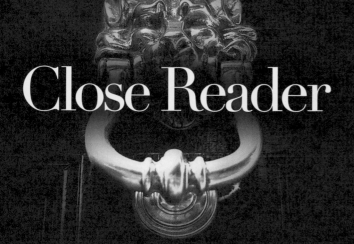

Houghton
Mifflin
Harcourt

Close Reader

GRADE 12

Program Consultants:

Kylene Beers

Martha Hougen

Carol Jago

William L. McBride

Erik Palmer

Lydia Stack

Printed in the U.S.A.

ISBN 978-0-544-08841-2

8 9 10   1421   22 21 20 19 18 17 16

4500585396   B C D E F G

fyi Visit **hmhfyi.com**
hmhfyi.com for current articles and informational texts.

COLLECTION 3
Voices of Protest

COLLECTION 4
Seeking Justice, Seeking Peace

© Houghton Mifflin Harcourt Publishing Company • Image Credits: ©Steve Schapiro/Corbis; ©Rob Howard/Corbis

COLLECTION 5
Taking Risks

COLLECTION 6
Finding Ourselves in Nature

Visit hmhfyi.com
for current articles and
informational texts.

Becoming A Close Reader

READING THE TEXTS

Challenging literary and informational texts require close reading to understand and appreciate their meanings fully. These texts may have difficult language or complex structures that become clear only with careful study. To fully understand these demanding texts, you need to learn how to read and reread slowly and deliberately.

The Close Reader provides many opportunities to practice close reading. To become a close reader,

- read each text in the Close Reader slowly all the way through.
- take time to think about and respond to the READ and REREAD prompts that help focus your reading.
- cite specific textual evidence to support your analysis of the selection.

Your goal in close reading is to build useful knowledge as you analyze the author's message and appreciate the author's craft.

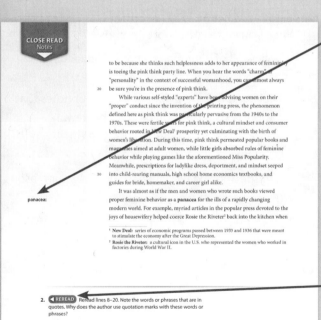

Background

This paragraph provides information about the text you are about to read. It helps you understand the context of the selection through additional information about the author, the subject, or the time period in which the text was written.

READ ▶

With practice, you can learn how to be a close reader. Questions and specific instructions at the beginning of the selection and on the bottom of the pages will guide your close reading of each text.

These questions and instructions

- refer to specific sections of the text.
- ask you to look for and mark up specific information in the text.
- prompt you to record inferences and text analysis in the side margins.
- help you begin to collect and cite text evidence.

Vocabulary

Critical vocabulary words appear in the margin throughout most selections. Consult a print or online dictionary to define the word on your own.

When you see a vocabulary word in the margin,

- write the definition of each vocabulary word in the margin.
- be sure your definition fits the context of the word as it is used in the text.
- check your definition by substituting it in place of the vocabulary word from the text. Your definition should make sense in the context of the selection.

◀ REREAD

To further guide your close reading, REREAD questions at the bottom of the page will

- ask you to focus on a close analysis of a smaller chunk of text.
- prompt you to analyze literary elements and devices, as well as the meaning and structure of informational text.
- help you go back into the text and "read between the lines" to uncover possible meanings and central ideas.

CLOSE READ
Notes

> " *If only all women behaved like our Ideal Woman . . . then everything would be fine.* "

her hubby came home from the war and expected his factory job back. During the early cold war years, some home economics texts seemed to suggest that knowing how to make hospital corners and a good tuna casserole were the only things between Our Way of Life and communist incursion. It was patriotic to
40 be an exemplary housewife. And pink-thinking experts of the sixties and seventies, trying to maintain this ideal, churned out reams of pages that countered the onrushing tide of the women's movement. If only all women behaved like our Ideal Woman, the experts seemed to say through the years, then everything would be fine.

You might even say that the "problem with no name" that Betty Friedan wrote about in *The Feminine Mystique* (1963) was a virulent strain of pink-thinkitis. After all, according to Friedan, "the problem" was in part engendered by the experts' insistence that women "could desire no greater destiny than to glory in their own femininity"—a pink think **credo.**   credo:
50 The pink think of the 1940s to 1970s held that femininity was necessary for catching and marrying a man, which was in turn a prerequisite for childbearing—the ultimate feminine fulfillment. This resulted in little girls playing games like Mystery Date³ long before they were ever interested in boys. It made home economics a high school course and college major, and suggested a teen girl's focus should be on dating and getting a boyfriend. It made beauty,

³ **Mystery Date:** a board game marketed to girls aged 6–14. The object of the game was to be ready for a date by assembling three matching cards to make an outfit appropriate for the date.

4. ◀ REREAD AND DISCUSS Reread lines 21–44. With a small group, identify and discuss Peril's central idea in these paragraphs.

5. READ ▶ As you read lines 45–65, continue to cite textual evidence.
   - In the margin, explain in your own words what the author means by "pink-thinkitis."
   - Underline text that describes other principles of "pink think."

35

CLOSE READ
Notes

mandatory:

charm, and submissive behavior of **mandatory** importance to women of all ages in order to win a man's attention and hold his interest after marriage. It promoted motherhood and housewifery as women's only meaningful career,
60 and made sure that women who worked outside the home brought "feminine charm" to their workplaces lest a career make them too masculine.

Not that pink think resides exclusively alongside antimacassars⁴ and 14.4 modems in the graveyard of outdated popular culture: Shoes, clothing, and movie stars may go in and out of style with astounding rapidity, but attitudes have an unnerving way of hanging around long after they've outlived their usefulness—even if they never had any use to begin with.

⁴ **antimacassars:** small cloths placed over the arms of furniture such as chairs or couches to prevent wear or soiling.

6. ◀ REREAD Reread lines 61–65. Why does Peril use the phrase "the graveyard of outdated popular culture" to refer to pink think?

_____
_____

SHORT RESPONSE

Cite Text Evidence Review your reading notes to identify elements of Peril's style. What words and phrases best suggest her perspective, or point of view, on pink think? **Cite textual evidence** in your response.

_____
_____
_____
_____
_____
_____
_____
_____
_____
_____
_____

36

◀ REREAD AND DISCUSS

These prompts encourage you to work with a partner or in a small group to discuss specific events, details, statements, and evidence from the text. These discussions will allow you to acquire and share knowledge about the texts you are reading.

As you engage in these discussions,

- be sure to cite specific text evidence in support of your statements.

- pose questions and integrate your ideas with the ideas of others.

- collaborate to reach a consensus or call attention to evidence that might have been missed or misinterpreted.

- acknowledge the views of others and be ready to modify your own thinking.

SHORT RESPONSE

At the end of each text, you will have an opportunity to sum up your thinking by completing a Short Response. The Short Response represents a place to convey some of the ideas you have developed through close reading of the text.

When you write your Short Response,

- review all of your margin notes and REREAD answers.

- circle or highlight evidence from your notes that supports your position or point of view.

- clearly state your point of view and support it with reasons.

- cite specific text evidence to support your reasons.

Chasing Success

Chasing Success

"If your success is not on your own terms, if it looks good to the world but does not feel good in your heart, it is not success at all."

—Anna Quindlen

Background *"Kewauna's Ambition" is an excerpt from* **Paul Tough's** *book* How Children Succeed: Grit, Curiosity, and the Hidden Power of Character. *In his research for this book, Tough met Kewauna Lerma, a 17-year-old student in a program called OneGoal, which works with high schools in Chicago to help at-risk students by teaching them noncognitive skills such as grit and self-control. Kewauna had a chaotic childhood, and she was homeless for a while. When she was 15, she was arrested for punching a police officer. But after a family intervention, Kewauna started working harder at school. With the help of OneGoal teacher Michele Stefl, Kewauna graduated high school and enrolled in college.*

Kewauna's Ambition

FROM **HOW CHILDREN SUCCEED**

Nonfiction by Paul Tough

CLOSE READ
Notes

1. **READD** ▶ As you read lines 1–30, begin to collect and cite text evidence.

- Underline Kewauna's challenges.
- Circle key elements of Kewauna's strategy for success.
- In the margin, use your own words to describe each part of her strategy.

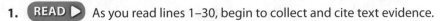

Her first fall at Western Illinois, Kewauna took introductory courses—English 100, Math 100, Sociology 100. None of them was easy for her, but the course she found most challenging was Biology 170, Introduction to Health Careers. The professor was a popular lecturer, so the class was pretty full, and most of the students were upperclassmen. On the first day of class, Kewauna did what Michele Stefl had recommended: she politely introduced herself to the professor before class, and then she sat in the front row, which until Kewauna sat down was occupied entirely by white girls. The other African American students all tended to sit at the back, which disappointed Kewauna.
10 ("That's what they *expect* you to do," she said when we talked by phone that fall. "Back in the civil rights movement, if they told you you had to sit in the back, you wouldn't do it.")

Her biology professor used a lot of scientific terms in his lectures that Kewauna wasn't familiar with. So she came up with a strategy: every time he used a word she didn't understand, she wrote it down and put a red star next to it. At the end of the class, she waited until all the other students who wanted to talk to the professor had taken their turns, and then she went through each red-starred word with him, one by one, asking him to explain them.

Kewauna spent a lot of time interacting with all her professors, in fact. She
20   was a regular at office hours, and she e-mailed them whenever she wasn't clear
on assignments. She also tried to make one or two acquaintances among the
students in each of her classes, so that if she needed help with homework and
couldn't reach the professor, she'd have someone to ask. Through her
freshman-support program, she found a writing tutor—she had always had
"grammar issues," she told me, as well as trouble with spelling and
punctuation—and she made a practice of going over with her tutor every paper
she wrote before handing it in. Finally, in December, she felt she had
internalized enough about comma splices and dependent clauses, and she
handed in her final English paper without going over it with the writing tutor.
30   She got an A.

Still, it was a difficult semester for Kewauna. She was always short of
money and had to economize everywhere she could. At one point, she ran out
of money on her meal card and just didn't eat for two days. She was studying
all the time, it felt like. Every paper was a challenge, and at the end of the
semester, she stayed up practically all night, three nights in a row, studying for
finals. But her hard work was reflected in her final grades that semester: two B
pluses, one A, and, in biology, an A plus. When I spoke to her a few days before
Christmas, she sounded a bit depleted, but proud too. "No matter how
overwhelming it is, no matter how exhausting it is, I'm not going to give up,"
40   she said. "I'm never the type to give up. Even when I played hide-and-go-seek
when I was little, I would be outside till eight o'clock, until I found everyone. I
don't give up on nothing, no matter how hard."

2. ◀ **REREAD**   Reread lines 5–12. Why do you think Kewauna is disappointed
that the other African American girls sat in the back? Support your answer with
explicit textual evidence.

_____

_____

_____

3. **READ** ▷   Read lines 31–50. Circle what the author says most impressed him
about Kewauna. In the margin explain why, in your own words.

4. ◀ **REREAD AND DISCUSS**   Reread lines 31–50. With a small group, discuss
why Kewauna was successful. What central idea does Tough make about
Kewauna's success in these lines?

There were still seven semesters to go, lots of time for things to go wrong, for setbacks and mistakes and crises. But Kewauna seemed certain of where she was heading and why—almost unnervingly so. What was most remarkable to me about Kewauna was that she was able to marshal her **prodigious** noncognitive capacity—call it grit, conscientiousness, resilience, or the ability to delay gratification—all for a distant prize that was, for her, almost entirely theoretical. She didn't actually *know* any business ladies with briefcases

50 downtown; she didn't even know any college graduates except her teachers.

Not all of Kewauna's fellow OneGoal students are going to take to the deal with the same **conviction**. And it won't be clear for another couple of years whether the leadership skills Kewauna and her classmates were taught are powerful enough to get them through four years of college. But so far, OneGoal's overall persistence numbers are quite good. Of the 128 students, including Kewauna, who started OneGoal as juniors at six Chicago high schools in the fall of 2009, ninety-six were enrolled in four-year colleges as of March 2012. Another fourteen were enrolled in two-year colleges, for an overall college-persistence total of 85 percent. Which left only nineteen

60 students who had veered off the track to a college degree: twelve who left OneGoal before the end of high school, two who joined the military after high school, two who graduated from high school but didn't enroll in college, and three who enrolled in college but dropped out in their first six months. The numbers are less stellar but still impressive for the pilot-program cohort,[1] students for whom OneGoal was a weekly afterschool class. Three years out of high school, 66 percent of the students who enrolled in the program as high-school juniors are still enrolled in college. Those numbers grow more significant when you recall that OneGoal teachers are deliberately selecting struggling students who seem especially unlikely to go to college.

70 Jeff Nelson[2] would be the first to admit that what he has created is far from a perfect solution for the widespread dysfunction of the country's human-capital[3] pipeline. Ideally, we should have in place an education and social-

---

[1] **cohort:** a group of individuals having a statistical factor (as age or class membership) in common in a demographic study.

[2] **Jeff Nelson:** co-founder and CEO of OneGoal.

[3] **human capital:** skills, training, and experience that make an employee valuable in the marketplace.

prodigious :

conviction:

5. **READ** ▶ As you read lines 51–78, summarize what you learn about OneGoal in the margin.

support system that produces teenagers from the South Side who *aren't* regularly two or three or four years behind grade level. For now, though, OneGoal and the theories that underlie it seem like a most valuable intervention, a program that, for about fourteen hundred dollars a year per student, regularly turns underperforming, undermotivated, low-income teenagers into successful college students.

6. **◄ REREAD** Reread lines 67–78. How does Tough think OneGoal might be improved? Support your answer with explicit textual evidence.

_____

_____

_____

_____

_____

SHORT RESPONSE

Cite Text Evidence Identify two of Tough's central ideas, and show how he supports them. Review your reading notes, and be sure to **cite text evidence** from the essay in your response.

_____

_____

_____

_____

_____

_____

_____

_____

_____

_____

Background *Title IX, part of the Educational Amendments of 1972, makes it illegal to exclude anyone from participating in any government-funded educational program or activity based on gender. Some people argue that this legislation should put a permanent end to single-sex education in public schools. However, in 2001, senators Kay Bailey Hutchison (R-TX) and Barbara Mikulski (D-MD) worked with other legislators to introduce an amendment to establish the legality of single-sex education offerings in public schools. Recently, they have had to defend their amendment. The following article appeared in* The Wall Street Journal *on October 16, 2012.*

A Right to Choose Single-Sex Education

Opinion by Kay Bailey Hutchison and Barbara Mikulski

CLOSE READ
Notes

1. **READD ▷** As you read lines 1–33, begin to collect and cite text evidence.

   • In the margin, restate the authors' position in lines 7–12.
   • Underline their claims (lines 13–33).
   • Circle opposing viewpoints.

Education proponents across the political **spectrum** were dismayed by recent attempts to eradicate the single-gender options in public schools in Virginia, West Virginia, Alabama, Mississippi, Maine and Florida. We were particularly troubled at efforts to **thwart** education choice for American students and their families because it is a cause we have worked hard to advance.

    Studies have shown that some students learn better in a single-gender environment, particularly in math and science. But federal regulations used to prevent public schools from offering that option. So in 2001 we joined with 10   then-Sen. Hillary Clinton and Sen. Susan Collins to author legislation that allowed public schools to offer single-sex education. It was an epic bipartisan[1] battle against entrenched bureaucracy, but well worth the fight.

spectrum:

thwart:

---

[1] **bipartisan:** representing, made up of, or organized by members of two political parties.

Since our amendment passed, thousands of American children have benefited. Now, though, some civil libertarians are claiming that single-sex public-school programs are discriminatory and thus illegal.

To be clear: The 2001 law did not require that children be educated in single-gender programs or schools. It simply allowed schools and districts to offer the choice of single-sex schools or classrooms, as long as opportunities were equally available to boys and girls. In the vast and growing realm of

20   education research, one central **tenet** has been confirmed repeatedly: Children learn in different ways. For some, single-sex classrooms make all the difference.

Critics argue that these programs promote harmful gender stereotypes. Ironically, it is exactly these stereotypes that the single-sex programs seek to eradicate.

As studies have confirmed—and as any parent can tell you—negative gender roles are often sharpened in coeducational environments. Boys are more likely, for instance, to buy into the notion that reading isn't masculine when they're surrounded by (and showing off for) girls.

Girls, meanwhile, have made so much progress in educational achievement

30   that women are overrepresented in postgraduate education. But they still lag in the acquisition of bachelor's and graduate degrees in math and the sciences. It has been demonstrated time and again that young girls are more willing to ask and answer questions in classrooms without boys.

A 2008 Department of Education study found that "both principals and teachers believed that the main benefits of single-sex schooling are decreasing distractions to learning and improving student achievement." The gender slant—the math-is-for-boys, home-EC-is- for-girls trope—is eliminated.

In a three-year study in the mid-2000s, researchers at Florida's Stetson University compared the performance of single-gender and mixed-gender

40   classes at an elementary school, controlling for the likes of class sizes,

tenet:

2. **◄ REREAD AND DISCUSS** Reread lines 7–15. With a small group, discuss your initial responses to the argument. Examine the strengths and weaknesses of their claims. Cite specific examples from the text to support your view.

3. **READ ▷** As you read lines 34–71, continue to cite textual evidence.

- Circle statistics provided as evidence, and underline the sources of these statistics.
- In the margin, restate the conclusion (lines 64–71).

> *No one is arguing that single-sex education is the best option for every student.*

demographics and teacher training. When the children took the Florida Comprehensive Assessment Test (which measures achievement in math and literacy, for instance), the results were striking: Only 59% of girls in mixed classes were scored as proficient, while 75% of girls in single-sex ones achieved proficiency. Similarly, 37% of boys in coeducational classes scored proficient, compared with 86% of boys in the all-boys classes.

Booker T. Washington High School in Memphis, Tenn., the winner of the 2011 Race to the Top High School Commencement Challenge, went to a 81.6% graduation rate in 2010 from a graduation rate of 55% in 2007.
50 Among the changes at the school? Implementing all-girls and all-boys freshman academies.

In Dallas, the all-boys Barack Obama Leadership Academy opened its doors last year. There is every reason to believe it will follow the success of the first all-girls public school, Irma Rangel Young Women's Leadership School, which started in 2004. Irma Rangel, which has been a Texas Education Agency Exemplary School since 2006, also took sixth place at the Dallas Independent School District's 30th Annual Mathematics Olympiad that year.

No one is arguing that single-sex education is the best option for every student. But it is preferable for some students and families, and no one has the
60 right to deny them an option that may work best for a particular child. Attempts to eliminate single-sex education are equivalent to taking away students' and parents' choice about one of the most fundamentally important aspects of childhood and future indicators of success—a child's education.

America once dominated educational attainment among developed countries, but we have fallen disastrously in international rankings. As we seek ways to offer the best education for all our children, in ways that are better tailored to their needs, it seems not just counterproductive but damaging to reduce the options. Single-sex education in public schools will continue to be a voluntary choice for students and their families. To limit or eliminate single-sex education is irresponsible. To take single-sex education away from students who stand to benefit is unforgivable.

70

4. **◄ REREAD** Reread lines 34–71. Make notes in the margin for the following.

• Evaluate the strength of the evidence presented.
• Restate in the margin the authors' positions in lines 58–63.
• Explain the appeal made in the final pararaph.

SHORT RESPONSE

Cite Text Evidence Explain whether or not the authors convinced you of the value of same-sex education. Review your reading notes and evaluate the strength and effectiveness of the claims and evidence presented. **Cite text evidence** to support your response.

_____

_____

_____

_____

_____

_____

_____

_____

Background Penelope Lively *was born in Cairo, Egypt, in 1933. At the age of twelve she moved to England, where she attended The Downs, a boarding school. "I was excruciatingly unhappy for four years," Lively says of her boarding school experience. She also notes, "The school was rigorously devoted to the improvement of its girls' lacrosse and netball." Boarding schools are fairly common in England. It is sometimes argued that expensive and exclusive boarding schools perpetuate an "old boy network" of social entitlement in English society.*

Next Term, We'll Mash You

Short Story by Penelope Lively

1. **READE** ▶ As you read lines 1–33, begin to collect and cite text evidence.

   • Underline descriptive words and phrases in lines 1–7.
   • In the margin, describe the mood of the first paragraph.
   • Underline some of the descriptive words in lines 29–33.
   • In the margin, describe your impression of the school.

Inside the car it was quiet, the noise of the engine even and **subdued**, the air just the right temperature, the windows tight-fitting. The boy sat on the back seat, a box of chocolates, unopened, beside him, and a comic, folded. The trim Sussex[1] landscape flowed past the windows: cows, white-fenced fields, highly priced period houses. The sunlight was glassy, remote as a colored photograph. The backs of the two heads in front of him swayed with the motion of the car.

His mother half-turned to speak to him. "Nearly there now, darling."

The father glanced downwards at his wife's wrist. "Are we all right
10 for time?"

"Just right. Nearly twelve."

''I could do with a drink. Hope they lay something on."[2]

"I'm sure they will. The Wilcoxes say they're awfully nice people. Not really the schoolmaster-type at all, Sally says."

subdued:

---

[1] **Sussex:** a county on the southeast coast of England.
[2] **lay something on:** have a reception with drinks and/or snacks.

The man said, "He's an Oxford chap."

"Is he? You didn't say."

"Mmn."

"Of course, the fees are that much higher than the Seaford place."

"Fifty quid[3] or so. We'll have to see."

20   The car turned right, between white gates and high, dark, tight-clipped hedges. The whisper of the road under the tires changed to the crunch of gravel. The child, staring sideways, read black lettering on a white board:

"St. Edward's Preparatory School. Please Drive Slowly." He shifted on the seat, and the leather sucked at the bare skin under his knees, stinging.

The mother said, " It's a lovely place. Those must be the playing fields. Look, darling, there are some of the boys." She clicked open her handbag, and the sun caught her mirror and flashed in the child's eye; the comb went through her hair and he saw the grooves it left, neat as distant ploughing.

"Come on, then, Charles, out you get."

30   The building was red brick, early nineteenth century, spreading out long arms in which windows glittered blackly. Flowers, trapped in neat beds, were alternate red and white. They went up the steps, the man, the woman, and the child two paces behind.

The woman, the mother, smoothing down a skirt that would be ridged from sitting, thought: I like the way they've got the maid all done up properly. The little white apron and all that. She's foreign, I suppose. Au pair.[4] Very nice. If he comes here, there'll be Speech Days and that kind of thing. Sally Wilcox says it's quite dressy—she got that cream linen coat for coming down here. You can see why it costs a bomb. Great big grounds and only an hour and a half
40   from London.

---

[3] **quid:** slang for pounds, British monetary unit.

[4] **au pair:** foreign person who does domestic work for room and board and for an opportunity to learn the language of her employers.

---

2. ◀ REREAD Reread lines 19–33. Do you think Charles is likely to agree with his mother that, "It's a lovely place"? Support your inference with explicit textual evidence.

_____

_____

3. READ ▶ As you read lines 34–111, continue to cite textual evidence.

• Circle the parents' unspoken thoughts.

• In the margin, make inferences based on the parents' thoughts.

They went into a room looking out into a terrace. Beyond, dappled lawns, gently shifting trees, black and white cows grazing behind iron railings. Books, leather chairs, a table with magazines—*Country Life, The Field, The Economist.* "Please, if you would wait here. The Headmaster won't be long."

Alone, they sat, inspected. "I like the atmosphere, don't you, John?"

"Very pleasant, yes." Four hundred a term, near enough. You can tell it's a cut above the Seaford place, though, or the one at St. Albans. Bob Wilcox says quite a few City people send their boys here. One or two of the merchant bankers, those kind of people. It's the sort of contact that would do no harm at
50 all. You meet someone, get talking at a cricket match or what have you . . . Not at all a bad thing.

"All right, Charles? You didn't get sick in the car, did you?"

The child had black hair, slicked down smooth to his head. His ears, too large, jutted out, transparent in the light from the window, laced with tiny, delicate veins. His clothes had the shine and crease of newness. He looked at the books, the dark brown pictures, his parents, said nothing.

"Come here, let me tidy your hair."

The door opened. The child hesitated, stood up, sat, then rose again with his father.

60 "Mr. and Mrs. Manders? How very nice to meet you—I'm Margaret Spokes, and will you please forgive my husband who is tied up with some wretch who broke the cricket pavilion window and will be just a few more minutes. We try to be organized but a schoolmaster's day is always just that bit unpredictable. Do please sit down and what will you have to revive you after that beastly drive? You live in Finchley,[5] is that right?"

"Hampstead[6] really," said the mother. "Sherry would be lovely." She worked over the headmaster's wife from shoes to hairstyle, pricing and assessing. Shoes old but expensive—Russell and Bromley. Good skirt. Blouse could be Marks and Sparks—not sure. Real pearls. Super Victorian ring. She's not gone to any
70 particular trouble—that's just what she'd wear anyway. You can be confident, with a voice like that, of course. Sally Wilcox says she knows all sorts of people.

The headmaster's wife said, "I don't know how much you know about us. Prospectuses[7] don't tell you a thing, do they? We'll look round everything in a minute, when you've had a chat with my husband. I gather you're friends of the Wilcoxes, by the way. I'm awfully fond of Simon—he's down for Winchester, of course, but I expect you know that."

---

[5] **Finchley:** part of the London borough of Barnet.

[6] **Hampstead:** part of the London borough of Camden—and a much more desirable place to live.

[7] **prospectuses:** brochures.

The mother smiled over her sherry. Oh, I know that all right. Sally Wilcox doesn't let you forget that.

"And this is Charles? My dear, we've been forgetting all about you! In a
80 minute I'm going to borrow Charles and take him off to meet some of the boys because after all you're choosing a school for him, aren't you, and not for you, so he ought to know what he might be letting himself in for and it shows we've got nothing to hide."

The parents laughed. The father, sherry warming his guts, thought that this was an amusing woman. Not attractive, of course, a bit homespun, but impressive all the same. Partly the voice, of course; it takes a bloody expensive education to produce a voice like that. And other things, of course. Background and all that stuff.

"I think I can hear the thud of the Fourth Form coming in from games,
90 which means my husband is on the way, and then I shall leave you with him while I take Charles off to the common-room."

For a moment the three adults centered on the child, looking, judging. The mother said, "He looks so hideously pale, compared to those boys we saw outside."

"My dear, that's London, isn't it? You just have to get them out, to get some color into them. Ah, here's James. James—Mr. and Mrs. Manders. You remember, Bob Wilcox was mentioning at Sports Day . . ."

The headmaster reflected his wife's style, like paired cards in Happy Families. His clothes were mature rather than old, his skin well-scrubbed, his
100 shoes clean, his **geniality** untainted by the least condescension. He was genuinely sorry to have kept them waiting, but in this business one lurches from one minor crisis to the next . . . And this is Charles? Hello, there, Charles. His large hand rested for a moment on the child's head, quite extinguishing the thin, dark hair. It was as though he had but to clench his fingers to crush the skull. But he took his hand away and moved the parents to the window, to observe the mutilated cricket pavilion, with **indulgent** laughter.

And the child is borne away by the headmaster's wife. She never touches him or tells him to come, but simply bears him away like some relentless tide, down corridors and through swinging glass doors, towing him like a frail craft,
110 not bothering to look back to see if he is following, confident in the strength of magnetism, or obedience.

geniality:

indulgent:

4. ◀ **REREAD** Reread lines 52–59 and 79–111. What picture of Charles is emerging? What can you infer about how he feels about being at the school?

© Houghton Mifflin Harcourt Publishing Company

And delivers him to a room where boys are scattered among inky tables and rungless chairs and sprawled on a mangy carpet. There is a scampering, and a rising, and a silence falling, as she opens the door.

"Now this is the Lower Third, Charles, who you'd be with if you come to us in September. Boys, this is Charles Manders, and I want you to tell him all about things and answer any questions he wants to ask. You can believe about half of what they say, Charles, and they will tell you the most fearful lies about the food, which is excellent."

120   The boys laugh and groan; **amiable**, exaggerated groans. They must like the headmaster's wife: There is licensed repartee.[8] They look at her with bright eyes in open, eager faces. Someone leaps to hold the door for her, and close it behind her. She is gone.

amiable:

The child stands in the center of the room, and it draws in around him. The circle of children contracts, faces are only a yard or so from him; strange faces, looking, assessing.

Asking questions. They help themselves to his name, his age, his school. Over their heads he sees beyond the window an inaccessible world of shivering trees and high racing clouds and his voice which has floated like a feather in

130   the dusty schoolroom air dies altogether and he becomes mute, and he stands in the middle of them with shoulders humped, staring down at feet: grubby plimsolls[9] and kicked brown sandals. There is a noise in his ears like rushing water, a torrential din out of which voices boom, blotting each other out so that he cannot always hear the words. Do you? they say, and Have you? And What's your? and the faces, if he looks up, swing into one another in kaleidoscopic patterns and the floor under his feet is unsteady, lifting and falling.

And out of the noises comes one voice that is complete, that he can hear. "Next term, we'll mash you," it says. "We always mash new boys."

And a bell goes, somewhere beyond doors and down corridors, and

140   suddenly the children are all gone, clattering away and leaving him there with the heaving floor and the walls that shift and swing, and the headmaster's wife comes back and tows him away, and he is with his parents again, and they are getting into the car, and the high hedges skim past the car windows once more, in the other direction, and the gravel under the tires changes to black tarmac.

"Well?"

---

[8] **licensed repartee:** approved witty replies.
[9] **plimsolls:** sneakers.

5.   **READ ▶**   As you read lines 112–161, continue to cite textual evidence.

- Underline details that describe the room "where boys are scattered."
- Underline Charles's reactions to the other students.
- Circle the threat one student makes. In the margin, explain what you think this threat means and describe Charles's response.

"I liked it, didn't you?" The mother adjusted the car around her, closing windows, shrugging into her seat.

"Very pleasant, really. Nice chap."

"I liked him. Not quite so sure about her."

150   "It's pricey, of course."

"All the same . . ."

"Money well spent, though. One way and another."

"Shall we settle it, then?"

"I think so. I'll drop him a line."

The mother pitched her voice a notch higher to speak to the child in the back of the car.

"Would you like to go there, Charles? Like Simon Wilcox. Did you see that lovely gym, and the swimming pool? And did the other boys tell you all about it?"

160   The child does not answer. He looks straight ahead of him, at the road coiling beneath the bonnet of the car. His face is haggard with anticipation.

6.   ◀ **REREAD AND DISCUSS**   Reread lines 137–161. With a small group, make an inference about why Charles does not tell his parents about the boy's threat. How might the parents have reacted if Charles had told them? Use evidence from the text to support your opinions.

SHORT RESPONSE

Cite Text Evidence   Compare Charles's outlook on the school with that of his parents. What specific phrases does Lively use to build an understanding of what drives the characters? **Cite text evidence** to support your analysis.

_____

_____

_____

_____

_____

_____

_____

_____

_____

Gender Roles

Gender Roles

"Like it or not, today we are all pioneers. . . .
The old rules are no longer reliable guides to
work out modern gender roles."

—Stephanie Coontz

NARRATIVE POEM

The Pardoner's Tale
from The Canterbury Tales

Geoffrey Chaucer,

translated by **Nevill Coghill**

ESSAY

from Pink Think

Lynn Peril

Background Geoffrey Chaucer *(c. 1343–1400) is often called the father of English poetry, and* The Canterbury Tales, *a work he never completed, is considered one of the very greatest works in the English language. In the medieval church, a pardoner was a clergy member who had authority from the pope to grant indulgences—certificates of forgiveness—to people who showed great charity. In practice, however, many pardoners—such as Chaucer's pilgrim—were unethical and sold their certificates to make money for the church or themselves.*

The Pardoner's Tale
from The Canterbury Tales

Narrative Poem by Geoffrey Chaucer   translated by Nevill Coghill

CLOSE READ
Notes

1. **READD** ▶ As you read lines 1–22, begin to collect and cite text evidence.

- Underline clues that show that the Pardoner tries to deceive the people he preaches to.
- In the margin, explain why the Pardoner characterizes himself as a pigeon (lines 11–13).

The Pardoner's Prologue

"My lords," he said, "in churches where I preach
I cultivate a haughty kind of speech
And ring it out as roundly as a bell;
I've got it all by heart, the tale I tell.
5   I have a text, it always is the same
And always has been, since I learnt the game,
Old as the hills and fresher than the grass,
Radix malorum est cupiditas. . . .[1]

    "I preach, as you have heard me say before,
10   And tell a hundred lying mockeries[2] more.
I take great pains, and stretching out my neck
To east and west I crane about and peck
Just like a pigeon sitting on a barn.

---

[1] *Radix malorum est cupiditas:* Latin for "The love of money is the root of all evil" (1 Timothy 6:10).
[2] **mockeries:** false tales.

My hands and tongue together spin the yarn

15   And all my antics are a joy to see.

avarice:

The curse of **avarice** and cupidity

Is all my sermon, for it frees the pelf.[3]

Out come the pence,[4] and specially for myself,

For my exclusive purpose is to win

castigate:

20   And not at all to **castigate** their sin.

Once dead what matter how their souls may fare?

They can go blackberrying, for all I care! . . .

    "And thus I preach against the very vice

I make my living out of—avarice.

25   And yet however guilty of that sin

Myself, with others I have power to win

Them from it, I can bring them to repent;

But that is not my principal intent.

Covetousness is both the root and stuff

30   Of all I preach. That ought to be enough.

    "Well, then I give examples thick and fast

From bygone times, old stories from the past.

A yokel[5] mind loves stories from of old,

Being the kind it can repeat and hold.

35   What! Do you think, as long as I can preach

And get their silver for the things I teach,

That I will live in poverty, from choice?

That's not the counsel of my inner voice!

---

[3] **pelf:** riches.

[4] **pence:** pennies.

[5] **yokel:** rustic.

2. ◀ **REREAD** Reread lines 19–20. Paraphrase what the Pardoner says. What is his "exclusive purpose"?

_____

_____

3. **READ** ▷ As you read lines 23–57, continue to cite textual evidence.

- Underline text that reveals what the Pardoner really thinks of those to whom he sells forgiveness.

- Circle statements in which the Pardoner reveals his own character.

No! Let me preach and beg from kirk[6] to kirk

40 And never do an honest job of work,

No, nor make baskets, like St. Paul, to gain

A livelihood. I do not preach in vain.

There's no apostle I would **counterfeit**;   **counterfeit:**

I mean to have money, wool and cheese and wheat

45 Though it were given me by the poorest lad

Or poorest village widow, though she had

A string of starving children, all agape.

No, let me drink the liquor of the grape

And keep a jolly wench in every town!

50   "But listen, gentlemen; to bring things down

To a conclusion, would you like a tale?

Now as I've drunk a draft of corn-ripe ale,

By God it stands to reason I can strike

On some good story that you all will like.

55 For though I am a wholly vicious man

Don't think I can't tell moral tales. I can!

Here's one I often preach when out for winning. . . ."

―――――――――――――

[6] **kirk:** church.

4. ◄ REREAD Reread lines 50–57. In the margin, summarize the narrator's
    final comments of the prologue.

SHORT RESPONSE

Cite Text Evidence Irony is a contrast between expectations and reality.
What is ironic about the Pardoner? **Cite text evidence** in your response.

_____

_____

_____

_____

_____

_____

_____

_____

5.   **READD ▶** As you read lines 58–107, continue to cite textual evidence.

- In the margin, explain who the Pardoner's tale will be about and who has just been killed (lines 58–72).
- Underline descriptions of and warnings about Death.
- In the margin, explain how the descriptions given by the tavern-knave and the innkeeper personify Death (lines 73–89).

The Pardoner's Tale

It's of three rioters[7] I have to tell

Who, long before the morning service bell,

60   Were sitting in a tavern for a drink.

And as they sat, they heard the hand-bell clink

Before a coffin going to the grave;

One of them called the little tavern-knave[8]

And said "Go and find out at once—look spry!—

65   Whose corpse is in that coffin passing by;

And see you get the name correctly too."

"Sir," said the boy, "no need, I promise you;

Two hours before you came here I was told.

He was a friend of yours in days of old,

70   And suddenly, last night, the man was slain,

Upon his bench, face up, dead drunk again.

There came a privy[9] thief, they call him Death,

Who kills us all round here, and in a breath

He speared him through the heart, he never stirred.

75   And then Death went his way without a word.

He's killed a thousand in the present plague,[10]

And, sir, it doesn't do to be too vague

If you should meet him; you had best be wary.

Be on your guard with such an adversary,

80   Be primed to meet him everywhere you go,

That's what my mother said. It's all I know."

---

[7] **rioters:** rowdy people, revelers.

[8] **tavern-knave:** serving boy at an inn.

[9] **privy:** hidden, secretive.

[10] **plague:** Bubonic plague killed at least a quarter of the population of Europe in the mid-14th century.

The **publican** joined in with, "By St. Mary,
What the child says is right; you'd best be wary,
This very year he killed, in a large village

85   A mile away, man, woman, serf at tillage,
Page[11] in the household, children—all there were.
Yes, I imagine that he lives round there.
It's well to be prepared in these alarms,
He might do you dishonor." "Huh, God's arms!"

90   The rioter said, "Is he so fierce to meet?
I'll search for him, by Jesus, street by street.
God's blessed bones! I'll register a vow!
Here, chaps! The three of us together now,
Hold up your hands, like me, and we'll be brothers

95   In this affair, and each defend the others,
And we will kill this traitor Death, I say!
Away with him as he has made away
With all our friends. God's dignity! Tonight!"

    They made their bargain, swore with appetite,
100   These three, to live and die for one another
As brother-born might swear to his born brother.
And up they started in their drunken rage
And made towards this village which the page
And publican had spoken of before.

105   Many and grisly were the oaths they swore,
Tearing Christ's blessed body to a shred;
"If we can only catch him, Death is dead!"

———————
[11] **page:** boy servant.

publican:

6. (◀ REREAD) Reread lines 90–107. What does the rioters' response to the description of Death tell you about their characters? Cite evidence in your response.

_____

_____

_____

When they had gone not fully half a mile,
Just as they were about to cross a stile,
110　They came upon a very poor old man
Who humbly greeted them and thus began,
"God look to you, my lords, and give you quiet!"
To which the proudest of these men of riot
Gave back the answer, "What, old fool? Give place!
115　Why are you all wrapped up except your face?
Why live so long? Isn't it time to die?"

　　The old, old fellow looked him in the eye
And said, "Because I never yet have found,
Though I have walked to India, searching round
120　Village and city on my pilgrimage,
One who would change his youth to have my age.
And so my age is mine and must be still
Upon me, for such time as God may will.

　　"Not even Death, alas, will take my life;
125　So, like a wretched prisoner at strife
Within himself, I walk alone and wait
About the earth, which is my mother's gate,
Knock-knocking with my staff from night to noon
And crying, 'Mother, open to me soon!
130　Look at me, mother, won't you let me in?
See how I wither, flesh and blood and skin!
Alas! When will these bones be laid to rest?
Mother, I would exchange—for that were best—
The wardrobe in my chamber, standing there

7.　**READ** ▶ As you read lines 108–166, continue to cite textual evidence.

- In the margin, explain who the old man calls Mother and what he calls "my mother's gate" (lines 124–137).
- Circle the ominous words the old man speaks in lines 138–148.
- Underline the old man's instructions about where to find death (lines 149–166).

8.　◀ **REREAD AND DISCUSS**　Reread lines 108–116. With a small group, discuss the rioters' meeting with the old man. What is ironic about their attitudes toward death?

135   So long, for yours! Aye, for a shirt of hair[12]
    To wrap me in!' She has refused her grace,
    Whence comes the pallor of my withered face.

      "But it dishonored you when you began
    To speak so roughly, sir, to an old man,
140   Unless he had injured you in word or deed.
    It says in holy writ, as you may read,
    'Thou shalt rise up before the **hoary** head

hoary:

    And honor it.' And therefore be it said
    'Do no more harm to an old man than you,
145   Being now young, would have another do
    When you are old'—if you should live till then.
    And so may God be with you, gentlemen,
    For I must go whither I have to go."

      "By God," the gambler said, "you shan't do so,
150   You don't get off so easy, by St. John!
    I heard you mention, just a moment gone,
    A certain traitor Death who singles out
    And kills the fine young fellows hereabout.
    And you're his spy, by God! You wait a bit.
155   Say where he is or you shall pay for it,
    By God and by the Holy Sacrament!
    I say you've joined together by consent
    To kill us younger folk, you thieving swine!"

      "Well, sirs," he said, "if it be your design
160   To find out Death, turn up this crooked way
    Towards that grove, I left him there today
    Under a tree, and there you'll find him waiting.
    He isn't one to hide for all your prating.[13]
    You see that oak? He won't be far to find.
165   And God protect you that redeemed mankind,
    Aye, and amend you!" Thus that ancient man.

---

[12] **shirt of hair:** a rough shirt made of animal hair, worn to punish oneself for one's sins.
[13] **prating:** talking at great length; chattering.

At once the three young rioters began
To run, and reached the tree, and there they found
A pile of golden florins[14] on the ground,
170 New-coined, eight bushels of them as they thought.
No longer was it Death those fellows sought,
For they were all so thrilled to see the sight,
The florins were so beautiful and bright,
That down they sat beside the precious pile.
175 The wickedest spoke first after a while.
"Brothers," he said, "you listen to what I say.
I'm pretty sharp although I joke away.
It's clear that Fortune has bestowed this treasure
To let us live in jollity and pleasure.
180 Light come, light go! We'll spend it as we ought.
God's precious dignity! Who would have thought
This morning was to be our lucky day?

"If one could only get the gold away,
Back to my house, or else to yours, perhaps—
185 For as you know, the gold is ours, chaps—
We'd all be at the top of fortune, hey?
But certainly it can't be done by day.
People would call us robbers—a strong gang,
So our own property would make us hang.

---

[14]**florins:** coins.

---

9. **READ ▷** As you read lines 167–204, continue to cite textual evidence.

- In the margin, paraphrase what distracts the rioters from seeking Death.
- In the margin, summarize the plan the rioters make.
- Underline text evidence that supports your summary.

10. **◁ REREAD** Reread lines 167–182. What is ironic about this discovery? How is it different from what you expected?

_____

_____

_____

190   No, we must bring this treasure back by night

Some prudent way, and keep it out of sight.

And so as a solution I propose

We draw for lots and see the way it goes;

The one who draws the longest, lucky man,

195   Shall run to town as quickly as he can

To fetch us bread and wine—but keep things dark[15]—

While two remain in hiding here to mark

Our heap of treasure. If there's no delay,

When night comes down we'll carry it away,

200   All three of us, wherever we have planned."

He gathered lots and hid them in his hand

Bidding them draw for where the luck should fall.

It fell upon the youngest of them all,

And off he ran at once towards the town.

205   As soon as he had gone the first sat down

And thus began a **parley** with the other: parley:

"You know that you can trust me as a brother;

Now let me tell you where your profit lies;

You know our friend has gone to get supplies

210   And here's a lot of gold that is to be

Divided equally amongst us three.

Nevertheless, if I could shape things thus

So that we shared it out—the two of us—

Wouldn't you take it as a friendly act?"

---

[15]**keep things dark:** act in secret, without giving away what has happened.

11.   **READd** ▶ As you read lines 205–235, continue to cite textual evidence.

  • Underline words the first rioter uses to persuade the other of his plan.

  • In the margin, explain the plan the two rioters make (lines 223–235).

  • Underline text evidence that supports your explanation.

215   "But how?" the other said. "He knows the fact
          That all the gold was left with me and you;
          What can we tell him? What are we to do?"

          "Is it a bargain," said the first, "or no?
          For I can tell you in a word or so
220   What's to be done to bring the thing about."
          "Trust me," the other said, "you needn't doubt
          My word. I won't betray you, I'll be true."

          "Well," said his friend, "you see that we are two,
          And two are twice as powerful as one.
225   Now look; when he comes back, get up in fun
          To have a wrestle; then, as you attack,
          I'll up and put my dagger through his back
          While you and he are struggling, as in game;
          Then draw your dagger too and do the same.
230   Then all this money will be ours to spend,
          Divided equally of course, dear friend.
          Then we can gratify our lusts and fill
          The day with dicing[16] at our own sweet will."
          Thus these two miscreants[17] agreed to slay
235   The third and youngest, as you heard me say.

          The youngest, as he ran towards the town,
          Kept turning over, rolling up and down
          Within his heart the beauty of those bright
          New florins, saying, "Lord, to think I might
240   Have all that treasure to myself alone!
          Could there be anyone beneath the throne
          Of God so happy as I then should be?"

          ---

          [16] **dicing:** gambling with dice.
          [17] **miscreants:** evildoers, villains.

12.   ◀ REREAD AND DISCUSS   Reread lines 209–235. With a small group,
      discuss the frequent references to religion by all three rioters. In what ways
      do these references to religion connect the rioters to the Pardoner who tells
      the tale?

And so the Fiend, our common enemy,
Was given power to put it in his thought
245   That there was always poison to be bought,
And that with poison he could kill his friends.
To men in such a state the Devil sends
Thoughts of this kind, and has a full permission
To lure them on to sorrow and **perdition**;
250   For this young man was utterly content
To kill them both and never to repent.

      And on he ran, he had no thought to tarry,
Came to the town, found an **apothecary**
And said, "Sell me some poison if you will,
255   I have a lot of rats I want to kill
And there's a polecat too about my yard
That takes my chickens and it hits me hard;
But I'll get even, as is only right,
With vermin that destroy a man by night."

260   The chemist answered, "I've a preparation
Which you shall have, and by my soul's salvation
If any living creature eat or drink
A mouthful, ere he has the time to think,
Though he took less than makes a grain of wheat,
265   You'll see him fall down dying at your feet;
Yes, die he must, and in so short a while
You'd hardly have the time to walk a mile,
The poison is so strong, you understand."

perdition:

apothecary:

13. READ ▶ As you read lines 236–295, continue to cite textual evidence.

- Circle references to evil.
- Summarize the plan the youngest rioter makes.
- Underline text evidence in lines 239–251 that supports your summary.

This cursed fellow grabbed into his hand
270   The box of poison and away he ran
Into a neighboring street, and found a man
Who lent him three large bottles. He withdrew
And deftly poured the poison into two.
He kept the third one clean, as well he might,
275   For his own drink, meaning to work all night
Stacking the gold and carrying it away.
And when this rioter, this devil's clay,
Had filled his bottles up with wine, all three,
Back to rejoin his comrades sauntered he.

280   Why make a sermon of it? Why waste breath?
Exactly in the way they'd planned his death
They fell on him and slew him, two to one.
Then said the first of them when this was done,
"Now for a drink. Sit down and let's be merry,
285   For later on there'll be the corpse to bury."
And, as it happened, reaching for a sup,
He took a bottle full of poison up
And drank; and his companion, nothing loth,[18]
Drank from it also, and they perished both.

290   There is, in Avicenna's[19] long relation
Concerning poison and its operation,
Trust me, no ghastlier section to transcend
What these two wretches suffered at their end.
Thus these two murderers received their due,
295   So did the treacherous young poisoner too.

        O cursed sin! O blackguardly excess!
O treacherous homicide! O wickedness!
O gluttony that lusted on and diced! . . .

---

[18] **nothing loth:** not at all unwilling.
[19] **Avicenna's:** Avicenna was an 11th-century Islamic physician who wrote descriptions of
     various poisons and their effects.

14. ◀ REREAD   Reread lines 280–289. In the margin, explain how each rioter
meets his death, and the irony of their deaths.

Dearly beloved, God forgive your sin

300 And keep you from the vice of **avarice**!

My holy pardon frees you all of this,

Provided that you make the right approaches,

That is with sterling, rings, or silver brooches.

Bow down your heads under this holy bull![20]

305 Come on, you women, offer up your wool!

I'll write your name into my ledger; so!

Into the bliss of Heaven you shall go.

For I'll absolve you by my holy power,

You that make offering, clean as at the hour

310 When you were born. . . . That, sirs, is how I preach.

And Jesu Christ, soul's healer, aye, the leech[21]

Of every soul, grant pardon and relieve you

Of sin, for that is best, I won't deceive you.

One thing I should have mentioned in my tale,

315 Dear people. I've some relics[22] in my bale

And pardons too, as full and fine, I hope,

As any in England, given me by the Pope.

If there be one among you that is willing

To have my absolution for a shilling[23]

320 Devoutly given, come! and do not harden

Your hearts but kneel in humbleness for pardon;

Or else, receive my pardon as we go.

You can renew it every town or so

Always provided that you still renew

325 Each time, and in good money, what is due.

It is an honor to you to have found

A pardoner with his credentials sound

Who can absolve you as you ply the spur

In any accident that may occur.

avarice:

---

[20]**bull:** an official document from the pope.

[21]**leech:** a physician.

[22]**relics:** the remains of a saint.

[23]**shilling:** a coin worth twelve pence.

15. **READ ▶** As you read lines 296–340, continue to cite textual evidence.

- Circle examples of what the Pardoner offers his listeners.
- Underline the forms of payment he accepts.
- In the margin, summarize his final sales pitch.

330 For instance—we are all at Fortune's beck—
Your horse may throw you down and break your neck.
What a security it is to all
To have me here among you and at call
With pardon for the lowly and the great
335 When soul leaves body for the future state!
And I advise our Host here to begin,
The most enveloped of you all in sin.
Come forward, Host, you shall be the first to pay,
And kiss my holy relics right away.
340 Only a groat[24] Come on, unbuckle your purse!

---

[24]**groat:** a silver coin worth less than a shilling.

16. ◄ **REREAD** Reread lines 330–340. What motivation for the Pardoner's
telling his tale is revealed in these lines? Cite text evidence in your response.

_____

_____

_____

SHORT RESPONSE

Cite Text Evidence   Relate the story of the rioters to the goal of the
Pardoner. How does the tale of the three rioters help the Pardoner make sales?
Review your reading notes, and **cite text evidence** in your response.

_____

_____

_____

_____

_____

_____

_____

Background *Author* **Lynn Peril** *has been described as a mild-mannered civil servant by day, and a serious—but lighthearted—proponent of womens' rights all of the time. The following essay comes from the introduction to her book* Pink Think: Becoming a Woman in Many Uneasy Lessons, *"a pop-culture history of the perilous path to achieving the feminine ideal."*

from
Pink Think

Essay by Lynn Peril

1. **READ ▶** As you read lines 1–20, begin to collect and cite text evidence.

   - Underline text in the first paragraph that explains what *pink think* is.
   - Circle stereotypes of femininity.
   - In the margin, note language that hints at the writer's point of view.

Pink think is a set of ideas and attitudes about what **constitutes** proper female behavior; a groupthink that was consciously or not adhered to by advice writers, manufacturers of toys and other consumer products, experts in many walks of life, and the public at large, particularly during the years spanning the mid-twentieth century—but enduring even into the twenty-first century. Pink think assumes there is a standard of behavior to which all women, no matter their age, race, or body type, must aspire.

"Femininity" is sometimes used as a code word for this mythical standard, which suggests that women and girls are always gentle, soft, delicate, nurturing beings made of "sugar and spice and everything nice." But pink think is more than a stereotyped vision of girls and women as poor drivers who are afraid of mice and snakes, adore babies and small dogs, talk incessantly on the phone, and are incapable of keeping secrets. Integral to pink think is the belief that one's success as a woman is grounded in one's allegiance to such behavior. For example, a woman who fears mice isn't necessarily following the dictates of pink think. On the other hand, a woman who isn't afraid of mice but pretends

constitutes:

10

33

to be because she thinks such helplessness adds to her appearance of femininity is toeing the pink think party line. When you hear the words "charm" or "personality" in the context of successful womanhood, you can almost always
20   be sure you're in the presence of pink think.

While various self-styled "experts" have been advising women on their "proper" conduct since the invention of the printing press, the phenomenon defined here as pink think was particularly pervasive from the 1940s to the 1970s. These were fertile years for pink think, a cultural mindset and consumer behavior rooted in New Deal[1] prosperity yet culminating with the birth of women's liberation. During this time, pink think permeated popular books and magazines aimed at adult women, while little girls absorbed rules of feminine behavior while playing games like the aforementioned Miss Popularity. Meanwhile, prescriptions for ladylike dress, deportment, and mindset seeped
30   into child-rearing manuals, high school home economics textbooks, and guides for bride, homemaker, and career girl alike.

It was almost as if the men and women who wrote such books viewed proper feminine behavior as a **panacea** for the ills of a rapidly changing modern world. For example, myriad articles in the popular press devoted to the joys of housewifery helped coerce Rosie the Riveter[2] back into the kitchen when

panacea:

---

[1] **New Deal:** series of economic programs passed between 1933 and 1936 that were meant to stimulate the economy after the Great Depression.
[2] **Rosie the Riveter:** a cultural icon in the U.S. who represented the women who worked in factories during World War II.

2. **◄ REREAD** Reread lines 8–20. Note the words or phrases that are in quotes. Why does the author use quotation marks with these words or phrases?

_____

_____

_____

_____

3. **READ ▶** As you read lines 21–44, continue to cite textual evidence.

• Circle products from the 1940s and 1970s that contained pink think ideas.

• Underline examples of what women were expected to be like during the "early cold war years."

• In the margin on the next page, describe women's expected role.

> " *If only all women behaved like our Ideal Woman . . . then everything would be fine.* "

her hubby came home from the war and expected his factory job back. During the early cold war years, some home economics texts seemed to suggest that knowing how to make hospital corners and a good tuna casserole were the only things between Our Way of Life and communist incursion. It was patriotic to
40 be an exemplary housewife. And pink-thinking experts of the sixties and seventies, trying to maintain this ideal, churned out reams of pages that countered the onrushing tide of the women's movement. If only all women behaved like our Ideal Woman, the experts seemed to say through the years, then everything would be fine.

You might even say that the "problem with no name" that Betty Friedan wrote about in *The Feminine Mystique* (1963) was a virulent strain of pink-thinkitis. After all, according to Friedan, "the problem" was in part engendered by the experts' insistence that women "could desire no greater destiny than to glory in their own femininity"—a pink think **credo**.

credo:

50 The pink think of the 1940s to 1970s held that femininity was necessary for catching and marrying a man, which was in turn a prerequisite for childbearing—the ultimate feminine fulfillment. This resulted in little girls playing games like Mystery Date[3] long before they were ever interested in boys. It made home economics a high school course and college major, and suggested a teen girl's focus should be on dating and getting a boyfriend. It made beauty,

---

[3] **Mystery Date:** a board game marketed to girls aged 6–14. The object of the game was to be ready for a date by assembling three matching cards to make an outfit appropriate for the date.

---

4. ◀ **REREAD AND DISCUSS** Reread lines 21–44. With a small group, identify and discuss Peril's central idea in these paragraphs.

5. **READ** ▶ As you read lines 45–65, continue to cite textual evidence.

  • In the margin, explain in your own words what the author means by "pink-thinkitis."
  • Underline text that describes other principles of "pink think."

mandatory:

charm, and submissive behavior of **mandatory** importance to women of all ages in order to win a man's attention and hold his interest after marriage. It promoted motherhood and housewifery as women's only meaningful career, and made sure that women who worked outside the home brought "feminine 60 charm" to their workplaces lest a career make them too masculine.

Not that pink think resides exclusively alongside antimacassars[4] and 14.4 modems in the graveyard of outdated popular culture: Shoes, clothing, and movie stars may go in and out of style with astounding rapidity, but attitudes have an unnerving way of hanging around long after they've outlived their usefulness—even if they never had any use to begin with.

----

[4] **antimacassars:** small cloths placed over the arms of furniture such as chairs or couches to prevent wear or soiling.

6. **◀ REREAD**　Reread lines 61–65. Why does Peril use the phrase "the graveyard of outdated popular culture" to refer to pink think?

_____

_____

_____

SHORT RESPONSE

Cite Text Evidence　Review your reading notes to identify elements of Peril's style. What words and phrases best suggest her perspective, or point of view, on pink think? **Cite textual evidence** in your response.

_____

_____

_____

_____

_____

_____

_____

_____

_____

_____

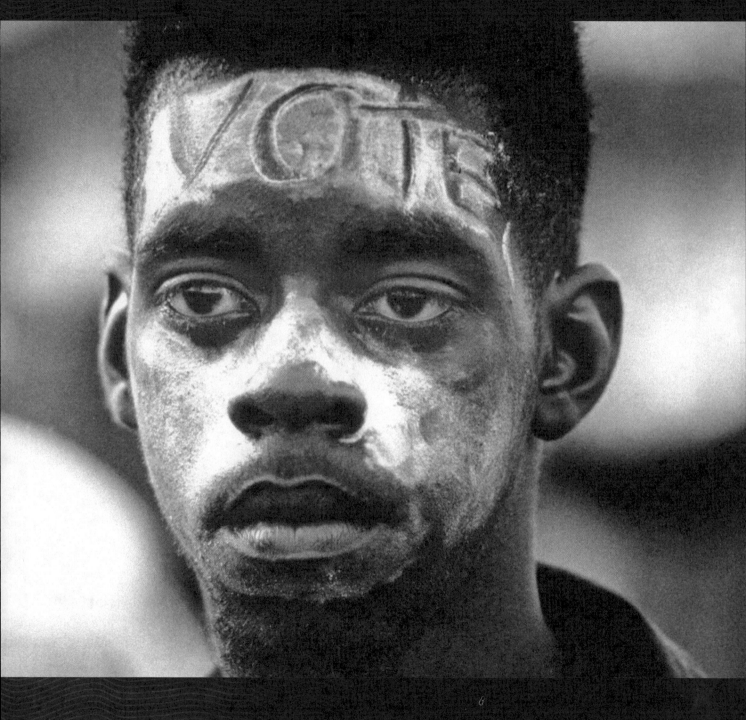

Voices of Protest

Voices of Protest

"We must always take sides. Neutrality helps the oppressor, never the victim."

—Elie Wiesel

Background Shirley Chisholm *(1924–2005) was born in New York City but spent her early years living with her maternal grandmother in Barbados. Committed to education and social justice, Chisholm began her career as a teacher, later becoming the first African American congresswoman, representing New York from 1969–1983. In 1972, despite what she termed "hopeless odds," she became the first African American woman to run for the office of U.S. President. Although unsuccessful in her presidential bid, she served seven terms in Congress, during which time she was a vocal opponent of social injustice, the draft, and the Vietnam War. She gave the following speech on March 26, 1969, to the House of Representatives.*

People and Peace, not Profits and War

Speech by Shirley Chisholm

CLOSE READ
Notes

1. **READE** As you read lines 1–24, begin to collect and cite text evidence.

- Circle the person being addressed at the beginning of the speech.
- Underline the argument Chisholm makes against defense spending in lines 5–8.
- Circle the loaded language Chisholm uses to describe the weapons in lines 5–8. In the margin, explain what she wants her listeners to understand.

Mr. Speaker, on the same day President Nixon announced he had decided the United States will not be safe unless we start to build a defense system against missiles, the Head Start[1] program in the District of Columbia was cut back for the lack of money.

As a teacher, and as a woman, I do not think I will ever understand what kind of values can be involved in spending $9 billion—and more, I am sure— on elaborate, unnecessary, and impractical weapons when several thousand disadvantaged children in the nation's capital get nothing.

When the new administration took office, I was one of the many
10 Americans who hoped it would mean that our country would benefit from the fresh **perspectives**, the new ideas, the different priorities of a leader who had no part in the mistakes of the past. Mr. Nixon had said things like this: "If our cities are to be livable for the next generation, we can delay no longer in launching new approaches to the problems that beset them and to the tensions

perspectives:

---

[1] **Head Start:** a federal agency that offers educational programs for children age 3 to 5, and a variety of services for their families.

that tear them apart." And he said, "When you cut expenditures for education, what you are doing is shortchanging the American future."

But frankly, I have never cared too much what people say. What I am interested in is what they do. We have waited to see what the new administration is going to do. The pattern is now becoming clear. Apparently

20 launching those new programs can be delayed for a while, after all. It seems we have to get some missiles launched first. Recently the new secretary of commerce spelled it out. The secretary, Mr. Stans, told a reporter that the new administration is "pretty well agreed it must take time out from major social objectives" until it can stop inflation.

The new secretary of health, education, and welfare, Robert Finch, came to the Hill[2] to tell the House Education and Labor Committee that he thinks we should spend more on education, particularly in city schools. But, he said, unfortunately we cannot "afford" to, until we have reached some kind of honorable solution to the Vietnam War. I was glad to read that the

30 distinguished Member from Oregon [Mrs. Green] asked Mr. Finch this: "With the crisis in education, and the crisis in our cities, can we wait to settle the war? Shouldn't it be the other way around? Unless we can meet the crisis in education, we really can't afford the war."

_____

[2] **Hill:** Capitol Hill, the center of the United States federal government.

2. **◀ REREAD** Reread lines 9–24. How does Chisholm use inductive reasoning to support her argument? What conclusion does she draw from the evidence she presents?

_____

_____

_____

_____

_____

3. **READ ▶** As you read lines 25–51, continue to cite textual evidence.

- Underline the opposing viewpoint Chisholm references in lines 25–33, and restate it in the margin.
- Circle the repetitive phrase Chisholm uses in lines 42–51.
- Underline the loaded language Chisholm uses in lines 42–51.

Secretary of Defense Melvin Laird came to Capitol Hill, too. His mission was to sell the antiballistic missile[3] insanity to the Senate. He was asked what the new administration is doing about the war. To hear him, one would have thought it was 1968, that the former secretary of state was defending the former policies, that nothing had happened, a president had never decided not to run because he knew the nation would reject him in despair over this tragic war we have blundered into. Mr. Laird talked to being prepared to spend at least two more years in Vietnam.

Two more years. Two more years of hunger for Americans, of death for our best young men, of children here at home suffering the lifelong handicap of not having a good education when they are young. Two more years of high taxes collected to feed the cancerous growth of a Defense Department budget that now consumes two-thirds of our federal income.

Two more years of too little being done to fight our greatest enemies— poverty, prejudice, and neglect—here in our own country. Two more years of fantastic waste in the Defense Department and of penny pinching on social programs. Our country cannot survive two more years, or four, of these kinds of policies. It must stop this year—now.

Now, I am not a **pacifist**. I am deeply, unalterably opposed to this war in Vietnam. Apart from all other considerations—and there are many—the main

pacifist:

---

[3] **antiballistic missile:** a weapon that intercepts and destroys ballistic missiles.

4. **◀ REREAD** Reread lines 42–51. How does Chisholm's use of repetition and her use of loaded language contribute to the persuasive power of the speech? Support your answer with explicit textual evidence.

_____

_____

_____

_____

_____

_____

5. **READ ▶** As you read lines 52–73, continue to cite textual evidence. Underline the main argument the author makes about the need for ending the Vietnam War, and restate it in the margin.

fact is that we cannot squander the lives, the money, the energy that we need desperately here, in our cities, in our schools.

I wonder whether we cannot reverse our whole approach to spending. For years, we have given the military, the defense industry, a blank check. New weapons systems are dreamed up, billions are spent, and many times they are found to be impractical, inefficient, unsatisfactory, even worthless. What do we 60 do then? We spend more money on them. But with social programs, what do we do? Take the Job Corps.[4] Its failure has been mercilessly exposed and criticized. If it had been a military research and development project, they would have been ready to pour more billions after those that had been wasted on it.

The case of Pride, Inc.,[5] is interesting. This vigorous, successful black organization here in Washington, conceived and built by young, inner-city men, has been ruthlessly attacked by its enemies in the government, in this Congress. At least six auditors from the General Accounting Office were put to work investigating Pride. They worked seven months and spent more than 70 $100,000. They uncovered a fraud. It was something less than $2,100. Meanwhile, millions of dollars—billions of dollars, in fact—were being spent by the Department of Defense, and how many auditors and investigators were checking into their negotiated contract? Five.

We Americans have come to feel that it is our mission to make the world free. We believe that we are the good guys everywhere—in Vietnam, in Latin

---

[4] **Job Corps:** a federally funded free education and training program that helps young people learn a career, earn a high-school diploma or GED, and find a good job.

[5] **Pride, Inc.:** a program of food distribution for poor African Americans in Washington, DC, begun after the 1968 riots there.

---

6. **◄ REREAD AND DISCUSS** Reread lines 52–73. With a small group, discuss whether the evidence Chisholm presents is sufficient to support her conclusion that the government's money is unfairly spent.

7. **READ ▷** As you read lines 74–94,

- underline the inductive reasoning that Chisholm uses to support her claim in lines 84–94.

- circle the conclusion she draws from the evidence she presents.

- in the margin, restate her conclusion in your own words.

America, wherever we go. We believe that we are the good guys at home, too.
When the Kerner Commission[6] told white America what black America had
always known, that prejudice and hatred built the nation's slums, maintain
them, and profit by them, white America would not believe it. But it is true.
80 Unless we start to fight and defeat the enemies of poverty and racism in our
own country and make our talk of equality and opportunity ring true, we are
exposed as hypocrites in the eyes of the world when we talk about making
other people free.

I am deeply disappointed at the clear evidence that the number-one
priority of the new administration is to buy more and more weapons of war, to
return to the era of the Cold War, to ignore the war we must fight here—the
war that is not optional. There is only one way, I believe, to turn these policies
around. The Congress can respond to the mandate that the American people
have clearly expressed. They have said, "End this war. Stop the waste. Stop the
90 killing. Do something for your own people first." We must find the money to
"launch the new approaches," as Mr. Nixon said. We must force the
administration to rethink its distorted, unreal scale of priorities. Our children,
our jobless men, our deprived, rejected, and starving fellow citizens must come
first.

For this reason, I intend to vote "No" on every money bill that comes to the
floor of this House that provides any funds for the Department of Defense—
any bill whatsoever—until the time comes when our values and priorities have

---

[6] **Kerner Commission:** an 11-member commission established to investigate the causes of
the 1967 race riots in the U.S.

8. **◀ REREAD** Reread lines 74–83. What idea is Chisholm emphasizing by
repeating the term "good guys"?

_____

_____

_____

_____

_____

9. **READ ▶** As you read lines 95–105, continue to cite textual evidence.

• Underline Chisholm's promise to her listeners.
• Circle text explaining the reason she gives for her decision.
• Underline the parallel statements that Chisholm makes.

CLOSE READ
Notes

been turned rightside up again, until the monstrous waste and the shocking profits in the defense budget have been eliminated and our country starts to

100   use its strength, its tremendous resources, for people and peace, not for profits and war.

It was Calvin Coolidge, I believe, who made the comment that "the business of America is business." We are now spending $80 billion a year on defense. That is two-thirds of every tax dollar. At this time, gentlemen, the business of America is war, and it is time for a change.

10. **◄ REREAD** Reread lines 102–105. Then, restate Chisholm's final comment.

_____

_____

_____

SHORT RESPONSE

Cite Text Evidence   Evaluate Chisholm's speech against the Vietnam War. Did she convince you that the money being spent on the Vietnam War could be better spent on social programs, such as education? Review your reading notes and **cite text evidence** in your response.

_____

_____

_____

_____

_____

_____

_____

_____

Who Speaks for the 1%?

Article by Joel Stein

1. **READone** ▶ As you read lines 1–11, begin to collect and cite text evidence.

    • Circle the opening statement of the article.
    • In the margin, explain the verbal irony in lines 1–2.
    • Underline the use of exaggeration in lines 5–8, and in the margin, explain what the author is ridiculing.

CLOSE READ
Notes

I don't like the top 1% of anything. Intelligence? Boring! Fun? Exhausting! Thoughtfulness? Annoying! Hairiness? Too hairy!

So I get why the Occupy Wall Street protesters gained momentum with their slogan WE ARE THE 99%. Everyone loves the 99%. You can have a beer with the 99%. You can eat with your hands in front of the 99%. You can talk about TV shows with the 99% without them telling you that while they don't think there's anything wrong with TV, if they had one, they would watch it literally all the time, so it's better to just not keep one in the house.

But I've met some of the top 1%, and on average, they're interesting,
10 generous and charming. You know who is in the top 1%? Tom Hanks. You know who is in the bottom 99%? Not Tom Hanks.

It's not just that we admire the 1%. We need them. The 1% started Time Inc., creating my job. They founded Stanford, where I went to college. They funded Facebook and my mortgage. They created the Bill & Melinda Gates Foundation, bankrolled most great art, paid for medical research and created genius grants. No one has ever woken up early to gather around a TV to watch a wedding of two 99 percenters.

Part of the reason I'm defending the 1% is that while all the other journalists waste their time with the Occupy Wall Street losers, the 1% are
20 available for some serious networking. But when I started talking to them, I learned that for all their supposed power, they are now too afraid to stand up for themselves. When I asked Kathy Griffin[1] to explain why she and her fellow 1 percenters are a boon to society, she said, "I wouldn't touch that topic with a 10-foot pole made out of $100 bills I made from Suddenly Susan Season 2." Mark Cuban,[2] the billionaire owner of the Dallas Mavericks who isn't even afraid of NBA refs, said, "I think there are financial engineers that add no value and fit the Occupy Wall Street stereotypes. They are the 1% of the 1% that mess it up for everyone." In other words, Cuban is going with the rallying cry, "We are the 99.99%."

---

[1] **Kathy Griffin:** a popular comedienne who appeared on the TV show *Suddenly Susan*.
[2] **Mark Cuban:** American businessman and investor. As owner of the Dallas Mavericks, Cuban has been fined numerous times by the National Basketball Association (NBA) for critical statements about the league and its referees.

---

2. **◀ REREAD** Reread lines 9–11. Why does the author use Tom Hanks as an example of the 1%? How are these lines sarcastic? Support your answer with explicit textual evidence.

_____

_____

_____

_____

_____

3. **READ ▶** As you read lines 12–29, continue to cite textual evidence.

• Circle the author's references to himself in lines 12–17.

• In the margin, explain his point of view in lines 12–17.

• Underline the words and phrases in lines 18–29 that express judgment of others.

I get that we need someone to blame.

30 So I guess it's up to me to point out that all this anger about income inequality is misplaced because, unlike any other time in history, these days the 1% don't live that differently than the middle class does. Never before has $10 wine tasted so much like $1,000 bottles—and the $10 bottles come with pictures of cute animals! A $15,000 car breaks down as rarely as one that costs $250,000 and has far more cup holders. The middle class and the rich watch the same stuff on TV and in movie theaters, have equal access to Wikipedia and pay the same college graduates to do nothing but make us complicated coffee drinks. It is so difficult for the 1% to live differently that they have to collect art. Collecting art is so boring, there aren't any reality shows about it.

40 I get that we need someone to blame. Everyone loves the banker when they're borrowing and hates him when they have to pay him back. They also hate him when he claims to have mixed up the orange $500s with the light peach $100s and suddenly has a lot of cash even though he owns only Vermont and Oriental Avenues. I don't know a lot about banking. But I do not believe that the worldwide recession was caused by financial derivatives created by the 1% who tricked the innocent 99%. I believe it was created by the great wide middle class who took out loans to live out the techno-bling dream we deified in rap songs and reality TV. Credit-card debt went up 75% from 1997 to 2007. We're now a nation of really poor people with a lot of frequent-flier miles.

50 The Tea Party and Occupy Wall Street are both right: We need government to get smaller and bigger. I'd argue for slashing middle-class entitlements but also adding services for migrant workers and that new poverty-stricken

4. **REREAD AND DISCUSS** Reread lines 12–29. With a small group, discuss the author's use of examples from popular culture to advance his point of view. How do these examples add to the satire?

5. **READ** As you read lines 30–63, continue to cite textual evidence. Underline examples the author gives of the supposed similarities between the 1% and the middle class. In the margin, explain who he blames for income inequality.

Muppet, Lily, who has to live on the same street as a monster who shoves cookies into his mouth just to let them fall right out.

But even I, who scored only in the 95th percentile on my math SAT, know that we are not going to dig out of our nation's debt just by jacking up taxes on the 1%. Raising their tax rate won't change the overall debt that much. We are all going to have to pay more and take less. Except for Lily. That poor girl can have whatever she wants.

60   Until people calm down and realize that, we should do something nice for the besieged 1 percenters. Invite Mark Zuckerberg to join you on FarmVille. Let Rupert Murdoch listen to your voice mail. Watch that silly Oprah network. At least until they get through this hard time.

6. ◀ **REREAD** Reread lines 55–63. In the margin, explain who the author is making fun of, and why.

SHORT RESPONSE

Cite Text Evidence What do you think is the author's real point of view on the economic crisis? What is he really satirizing? Review your reading notes, and evaluate the author's style. **Cite evidence from the text** in your response.

_____

_____

_____

_____

_____

_____

_____

_____

_____

Elsewhere

Poem by Derek Walcott

1. **READD** As you read lines 1–12, begin to collect and cite text evidence.

- Circle each use of the word *somewhere*.
- Underline the example of personification in lines 5–8.
- In the margin, analyze how the image it creates contributes to the tone of the poem.

CLOSE READ
Notes

(For Stephen Spender)

Somewhere a white horse gallops with its mane
plunging round a field whose sticks
are ringed with barbed wire, and men
break stones or bind straw into ricks.

5   Somewhere women tire of the shawled sea's
weeping, for the fishermen's dories
still go out. It is blue as peace.
Somewhere they're tired of torture stories.

That somewhere there was an arrest.
10   Somewhere there was a small harvest
of bodies in the truck. Soldiers rest
somewhere by a road, or smoke in a forest.

Somewhere there is the conference rage
at an outrage. Somewhere a page
15   is torn out, and somehow the foliage
no longer looks like leaves but camouflage.

Somewhere there is a comrade,
a writer lying with his eyes wide open
on a mattress ticking, who will not read
20   this, or write. How to make a pen?

2.   **◄ REREAD** Reread lines 1–12. What is the speaker emphasizing by
repeating the word *somewhere*? How does the repetition of this word
choice affect the meaning and tone of the poem? Support your answer with
explicit textual evidence.

_____

_____

_____

_____

_____

_____

_____

3.   **READ ▶** As you read lines 13–20, continue to cite textual evidence.

• Circle the simile in lines 13–16.

• In the margin, explain the image that this simile creates.

• Underline the subject of lines 17–20. In the margin, state the point the poet is
making about this person.

> Somewhere there is a comrade . . . who will not read this, or write.

And here we are free for a while, but
elsewhere, in one-third, or one-seventh
of this planet, a summary rifle butt
breaks a skull into the idea of a heaven

25 where nothing is free, where blue air
is paper-frail, and whatever we write
will be stamped twice, a blue letter,
its throat slit by the paper knife of the state.

Through these black bars
30 hollowed faces stare. Fingers
grip the cross bars of these stanzas
and it is here, because somewhere else

4. ◀ **REREAD AND DISCUSS** With a small group, discuss the tone of the poem so far. What is the speaker's attitude toward the subject?

5. **READ** ▶ As you read lines 21–40, continue to cite textual evidence.
   • Circle what is happening "here," in line 21.
   • Underline what is happening "elsewhere."
   • In the margin, compare what is happening "here" with what is happening "elsewhere." What does this comparison say about freedom?

their stares fog into oblivion
thinly, like the faceless numbers
35 that bewilder you in your telephone
diary. Like last year's massacres.

The world is blameless. The darker crime
is to make a career of conscience,
to feel through our own nerves the silent scream
40 of winter branches, wonders read as signs.

---

6. ◄ REREAD As you reread lines 33–40,

• in the margin, explain the two images in lines 33–36.
• underline the personification in the last stanza.

SHORT RESPONSE

Cite Text Evidence Analyze the impact of specific word choices, including figurative and connotative meanings of words, on the meaning and tone of the poem. **Cite text evidence** in your response.

_____

_____

_____

_____

_____

_____

_____

_____

Seeking Justice, Seeking Peace

Seeking Justice, Seeking Peace

"Forgiving means abandoning your right to pay back the perpetrator in his own coin, but it is a loss which liberates the victim."

—Desmond Tutu

DRAMA

from The Tragedy of Hamlet   **William Shakespeare**
   Act 1. Scenes 1–2

SPEECH

Nobel Peace Prize
Acceptance Speech   **Wangari Maathai**

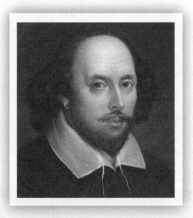

Background *Written by* **William Shakespeare,** The Tragedy of Hamlet *is considered one of the greatest dramas ever written. It's a political thriller, a murder mystery, and a tragic tale of vengeance. Set in Denmark, the play revolves around Prince Hamlet's quest for revenge. As the play opens, Hamlet's father has died and his uncle Claudius has swiftly married Hamlet's mother Gertrude and pronounced himself the new king. Horatio, Hamlet's friend, joins two guards at the castle wall.*

from
THE TRAGEDY OF
HAMLET

Drama by William Shakespeare

CLOSE READ
Notes

CHARACTERS

The Ghost

Hamlet, Prince of Denmark, son of the late King Hamlet and Queen Gertrude

Queen Gertrude, widow of King Hamlet, now married to Claudius

King Claudius, brother to the late King Hamlet

Polonius, councillor to King Claudius

Laertes, son of Polonius

Horatio, Hamlet's friend and confidant

COURTIERS AT THE DANISH COURT

Voltemand   **Cornelius**

DANISH SOLDIERS

Francisco   **Barnardo**

Marcellus

Place: Denmark

1. **READ** ▶ As you read lines 1–37, begin to collect and cite text evidence.

   • Underline clues that identify an important event that has already occurred.

   • In the margin, explain what the section reveals about the government or social structure of the country.

ACT I

Scene 1 • *A guard platform at Elsinore Castle.*

[*Enter* Barnardo *and* Francisco, *two sentinels.*]

Barnardo. Who's there?

Francisco. Nay, answer me. Stand and unfold[1] yourself.

Barnardo. Long live the King!

Francisco. Barnardo.

5   **Barnardo.** He.

Francisco. You come most carefully upon your hour.

Barnardo. 'Tis now struck twelve. Get thee to bed, Francisco.

Francisco. For this relief much thanks. 'Tis bitter cold,
And I am sick at heart.

10   **Barnardo.** Have you had quiet guard?

Francisco. Not a mouse stirring.

Barnardo. Well, good night.
If you do meet Horatio and Marcellus,
The rivals of my watch,[2] bid them make haste.

[*Enter* Horatio *and* Marcellus.]

15   **Francisco.** I think I hear them.—Stand ho! Who is there?

Horatio. Friends to this ground.

Marcellus. And liegemen to the Dane.[3]

Francisco. Give you good night.

Marcellus. O farewell, honest soldier. Who hath relieved you?

20   **Francisco.** Barnardo hath my place. Give you good night.

[Francisco *exits.*]

Marcellus. Holla, Barnardo.

Barnardo. Say, what, is Horatio there?

Horatio. A piece of him.

Barnardo. Welcome, Horatio.—Welcome, good Marcellus.

25   **Horatio.** What, has this thing appeared again tonight?

---

[1] **unfold:** identify.

[2] **rivals of my watch:** the others on guard duty with me.

[3] **liegemen to the Dane:** loyal subjects of the Danish king.

Barnardo. I have seen nothing.

Marcellus. Horatio says 'tis but our fantasy

And will not let belief take hold of him

Touching this dreaded sight twice seen of us.

30   Therefore I have entreated him along

With us to watch the minutes of this night,

That, if again this **apparition** come,   **apparition:**

He may approve our eyes⁴ and speak to it.

Horatio. Tush, tush, 'twill not appear.

Barnardo.   Sit down awhile,

35   And let us once again assail your ears,

That are so fortified against our story,

What we have two nights seen.

Horatio.   Well, sit we down,

And let us hear Barnardo speak of this.

Barnardo. Last night of all,

40   When yond same star that's westward from the pole

Had made his course t'illume that part of heaven

Where now it burns, Marcellus and myself,

The bell then beating one—

[*Enter* Ghost.]

Marcellus. Peace, break thee off! Look where it comes again.

45   **Barnardo.** In the same figure like the King that's dead.

Marcellus (*to* Horatio). Thou art a scholar. Speak to it, Horatio.

Barnardo. Looks he not like the King? Mark it, Horatio.

---

⁴ **approve our eyes:** confirm what we have seen.

2. ◀ REREAD   Reread lines 27–37. What conflicting opinions do Marcellus
    and Horatio express? What does Marcellus hope will change Horatio's view?

_____

_____

_____

3. READ ▶   As you read lines 38–73, continue to cite textual evidence.

   • Underline text that shows which man has changed his mind about the
     "apparition."

   • In the margin, explain how Shakespeare gives the events a dynamic pacing
     rather than just having characters present information.

Horatio. Most like. It harrows me with fear and wonder.

Barnardo. It would be spoke to.

Marcellus.   Speak to it, Horatio.

50 **Horatio.** What art thou that usurp'st⁵ this time of night,

Together with that fair and warlike form

In which the majesty of buried Denmark⁶

Did sometimes⁷ march? By heaven, I charge thee, speak.

Marcellus. It is offended.

Barnardo.   See, it stalks away.

55 **Horatio.** Stay! speak! speak! I charge thee, speak!

[Ghost *exits*.]

Marcellus. 'Tis gone and will not answer.

Barnardo. How now, Horatio, you tremble and look pale.

Is not this something more than fantasy?

What think you on 't?

60 **Horatio.** Before my God, I might not this believe

Without the sensible and true avouch⁸

Of mine own eyes.

Marcellus.   Is it not like the King?

Horatio. As thou art to thyself.

Such was the very armor he had on

65 When he the ambitious Norway⁹ combated.

So frowned he once when, in an angry parle,¹⁰

He smote the sledded Polacks on the ice.

'Tis strange.

Marcellus. Thus twice before, and jump¹¹ at this dead hour,

70 With martial stalk hath he gone by our watch.

---

⁵ **usurp'st:** unlawfully takes over.

⁶ **the majesty of buried Denmark:** the buried King of Denmark.

⁷ **sometimes:** formerly.

⁸ **avouch:** proof.

⁹ **Norway:** the king of Norway; Shakespeare often refers to the ruler of a country by the country's name.

¹⁰ **parle:** meeting with an enemy.

¹¹ **jump:** exactly.

---

4. **◄ REREAD** Reread lines 57–73. What mood has Shakespeare established so far? Cite textual evidence in your response.

_____

_____

_____

"*Is not this something more than fantasy?*"

Horatio. In what particular thought to work I know not,

But in the gross and scope of mine opinion

This bodes some strange eruption[12] to our state.

Marcellus. Good now, sit down, and tell me, he that knows,

75   Why this same strict and most observant watch

So nightly toils the subject of the land,[13]

And why such daily cast of **brazen** cannon

And foreign mart[14] for implements of war,

Why such impress[15] of shipwrights, whose sore task

80   Does not divide the Sunday from the week.

What might be toward[16] that this sweaty haste

Doth make the night joint laborer with the day?

Who is 't that can inform me?

Horatio.   That can I.

At least the whisper goes so: our last king,

85   Whose image even but now appeared to us,

Was, as you know, by Fortinbras of Norway,

Thereto pricked on by a most emulate pride,

Dared to the combat; in which our valiant Hamlet

(For so this side of our known world esteemed him)

90   Did slay this Fortinbras, who by a sealed compact,[17]

Well ratified by law and heraldry,

brazen:

---

[12] **eruption:** an outbreak, often of something evil.

[13] **subject of the land:** the ordinary Danish people.

[14] **mart:** trade.

[15] **impress:** forced service.

[16] **toward:** approaching, in preparation.

[17] **sealed compact:** prior agreement.

---

5. **READ** ▶ As you read lines 74–129, continue to cite textual evidence.

• Underline sentences that talk about the dead king of Norway, the elder Fortinbras.

• Circle text that refers to the dead king's son, the younger Fortinbras.

• In the margin, explain the connection between the ghost and King Hamlet.

Did forfeit, with his life, all those his lands

Which he stood seized of, to the conqueror.

Against the which a moiety competent[18]

95 Was gagèd[19] by our king, which had[20] returned

To the inheritance of Fortinbras

Had he been vanquisher, as, by the same comart

And carriage of the article designed, [21]

His fell to Hamlet. Now, sir, young Fortinbras,

100 Of unimproved mettle[22] hot and full,

Hath in the skirts of Norway here and there

Sharked up[23] a list of lawless resolutes

For food and diet to some enterprise

That hath a stomach in 't; which is no other

105 (As it doth well appear unto our state)

But to recover of us, by strong hand

And terms compulsatory, those foresaid lands

So by his father lost. And this, I take it,

Is the main motive of our preparations,

110 The source of this our watch, and the chief head

Of this posthaste and rummage in the land.

Barnardo. I think it be no other but e'en so.

portenteous:

Well may it sort that this **portentous** figure

Comes armed through our watch so like the king

115 That was and is the question of these wars.

Horatio. A mote it is to trouble the mind's eye.

In the most high and palmy state of Rome,

A little ere the mightiest Julius[24] fell,

The graves stood tenantless, and the sheeted dead

120 Did squeak and gibber in the Roman streets;

As stars with trains of fire and dews of blood,

Disasters in the sun; and the moist star,[25]

Upon whose influence Neptune's empire stands,

Was sick almost to doomsday with eclipse.

---

[18] **moiety competent:** equivalent portion.

[19] **gagéd:** pledged.

[20] **had:** would have.

[21] **comart and carriage of the article designed:** agreement.

[22] **unimproved mettle:** undisciplined character

[23] **sharked up:** gathered hastily.

[24] **the mightiest Julius:** Julius Caesar, ruler of ancient Rome, who was assassinated.

[25] **the moist star:** the Moon.

125 And even the like precurse of feared events,
As harbingers preceding still the fates
And prologue to the omen coming on,
Have heaven and earth together demonstrated
Unto our climatures²⁶ and countrymen.
[*Enter* Ghost.]

130 But soft, behold! Lo, where it comes again!
I'll cross it though it blast me.—Stay, illusion!
[*It spreads his arms.*]
If thou hast any sound or use of voice,
Speak to me.
If there be any good thing to be done

135 That may to thee do ease and grace to me,
Speak to me.
If thou art privy to thy country's fate,
Which happily²⁷ foreknowing may avoid,
O, speak!

140 Or if thou hast uphoarded in thy life
Extorted treasure in the womb of earth,
For which, they say, you spirits oft walk in death,
Speak of it.

_____
²⁶**climatures:** land.
²⁷**happily:** perhaps.

6. **◄ REREAD** Reread lines 116–129. What is the effect of including the references to Julius Caesar's assassination in ancient Rome? Cite textual evidence in your response.

_____

_____

_____

_____

7. **READ ►** As you read lines 130–181, continue to cite textual evidence.

• Underline the soldiers' attempts to engage the ghost and their descriptions of its actions.

• In the margin, explain what the soldiers want to learn from the ghost.

[*The cock crows.*]

                    Stay and speak!—Stop it, Marcellus.

Marcellus. Shall I strike it with my partisan?[28]

145 **Horatio.** Do, if it will not stand.

Barnardo. 'Tis here.

Horatio. 'Tis here.

[Ghost *exits.*]

Marcellus. 'Tis gone.

We do it wrong, being so majestical,

150 To offer it the show of violence,

For it is as the air, invulnerable,

And our vain blows malicious mockery.

Barnardo. It was about to speak when the cock crew.

Horatio. And then it started[29] like a guilty thing

155 Upon a fearful summons. I have heard

The cock, that is the trumpet to the morn,

Doth with his lofty and shrill-sounding throat

Awake the god of day, and at his warning,

Whether in sea or fire, in earth or air,

erring: 160 Th' extravagant and **erring** spirit hies

To his confine, and of the truth herein

This present object made probation.[30]

Marcellus. It faded on the crowing of the cock.

Some say that ever 'gainst that season comes

165 Wherein our Savior's birth is celebrated,

This bird of dawning singeth all night long;

And then, they say, no spirit dare stir abroad,

The nights are wholesome; then no planets strike,[31]

No fairy takes, nor witch hath power to charm,

170 So hallowed and so gracious is that time.

Horatio. So have I heard and do in part believe it.

But look, the morn in russet mantle clad

Walks o'er the dew of yon high eastward hill.

Break we our watch up, and by my advice

175 Let us impart what we have seen tonight

Unto young Hamlet; for, upon my life,

This spirit, dumb to us, will speak to him.

---

[28]**partisan:** a weapon.

[29]**started:** made a sudden movement.

[30]**made probation:** demonstrated.

[31]**no planets strike:** no planets put forth an evil influence.

Do you consent we shall acquaint him with it

As needful in our loves, fitting our duty?

180 **Marcellus.** Let's do 't, I pray, and I this morning know

Where we shall find him most convenient.

[*They exit.*]

Scene 2 • *A state room at the castle.*

[*Flourish. Enter* Claudius, *King of Denmark,* Gertrude *the Queen,* the Council, *as* Polonius, *and his son* Laertes, Hamlet, *with others, among them* Voltemand *and* Cornelius.]

King. Though yet of Hamlet our[32] dear brother's death

The memory be green, and that it us befitted

To bear our hearts in grief, and our whole kingdom

To be contracted in one brow of woe,

5 Yet so far hath discretion fought with nature

That we with wisest sorrow think on him

Together with remembrance of ourselves.

Therefore our sometime sister,[33] now our queen,

Th' imperial jointress[34] to this warlike state,

10 Have we (as 'twere with a defeated joy,

With an auspicious and a dropping eye,[35]

With mirth in funeral and with dirge in marriage,

In equal scale weighing delight and dole)

Taken to wife. Nor have we herein barred

15 Your better wisdoms, which have freely gone

With this affair along. For all, our thanks.

---

[32] **our:** the "royal we," referring to oneself.

[33] **our sometime sister:** my former sister-in-law.

[34] **jointress:** a woman who owns property with her husband.

[35] **an auspicious and a dropping eye:** one eye showing good fortune and the other showing sorrow.

8. ◀ **REREAD AND DISCUSS** Reread lines 171–181. In a small group, discuss how this last exchange of dialogue between Horatio and Marcellus advances the plot. Cite textual evidence in your discussion.

9. **READ** ▷ As you read Scene 2, lines 1–50, continue to cite text evidence.

- Underline examples of contradictory statements (lines 1–15).
- In the margin, tell what two events this set of contradictory elements describes.
- In the margin, explain what Claudius says that confirms what Horatio told the sentries earlier about Denmark.

Now follows that you know. Young Fortinbras,

Holding a weak supposal of our worth

Or thinking by our late dear brother's death

20   Our state to be disjoint and out of frame,

Colleagued with this dream of his advantage,

He hath not failed to pester us with message

Importing[36] the surrender of those lands

Lost by his father, with all bonds of law,

25   To our most valiant brother—so much for him.

Now for ourself and for this time of meeting.

Thus much the business is: we have here writ

To Norway, uncle of young Fortinbras,

Who, impotent and bedrid, scarcely hears

30   Of this his nephew's purpose, to suppress

His further gait herein, in that the levies,[37]

The lists, and full proportions are all made

Out of his subject;[38] and we here dispatch

You, good Cornelius, and you, Voltemand,

35   For bearers of this greeting to old Norway,

Giving to you no further personal power

To business with the King more than the scope

dilated: Of these **dilated** articles allow.

[*Giving them a paper.*]

Farewell, and let your haste commend your duty.

40   **Cornelius/Voltemand.** In that and all things will we show our duty.

King. We doubt it nothing. Heartily farewell.

[Voltemand *and* Cornelius *exit.*]

---

[36]**importing:** relating to.

[37]**levies:** gathered troops.

[38]**out of his subject:** from the King's own subjects.

---

10.   ◀ **REREAD**   Reread lines 17–38. One key theme of *Hamlet* is the nature of relationships between fathers and sons. What other father-son pairing seems to parallel that of Prince Hamlet and his father, King Hamlet?

_____

_____

_____

_____

And now, Laertes, what's the news with you?

You told us of some suit. What is 't, Laertes?

You cannot speak of reason to the Dane

45   And lose your voice. What wouldst thou beg, Laertes,

That shall not be my offer, not thy asking?

The head is not more native to the heart,

The hand more instrumental to the mouth,

Than is the throne of Denmark to thy father.

50   What wouldst thou have, Laertes?

Laertes.   My dread lord,

Your leave and favor to return to France,

From whence though willingly I came to Denmark

To show my duty in your coronation,

Yet now I must confess, that duty done,

55   My thoughts and wishes bend again toward France

And bow them to your gracious leave and pardon.

King. Have you your father's leave? What says Polonius?

Polonius. Hath, my lord, wrung from me my slow leave

By laborsome petition, and at last

60   Upon his will I sealed my hard consent.

I do beseech you give him leave to go.

King. Take thy fair hour, Laertes. Time be thine,

And thy best graces spend it at thy will.—

But now, my cousin³⁹ Hamlet and my son—

65   **Hamlet** [*aside*]. A little more than kin and less than kind.

King. How is it that the clouds still hang on you?

Hamlet. Not so, my lord; I am too much in the sun.

Queen. Good Hamlet, cast thy nighted color off,

And let thine eye look like a friend on Denmark.

70   Do not forever with thy vailèd lids

Seek for thy noble father in the dust.

Thou know'st 'tis common; all that lives must die,

Passing through nature to eternity.

---

³⁹**cousin:** kinsman.

11.   **READ ▶** As you read lines 51–86, continue to cite textual evidence.

• Underline the first words spoken by Hamlet, and in the margin explain why his first words might be delivered as an aside.

• In the margin, explain how King Claudius, the Queen, Prince Hamlet, and the dead King are related to one another.

Hamlet. Ay, madam, it is common.

Queen.   If it be,

75   Why seems it so particular with thee?

Hamlet. "Seems," madam? Nay, it is. I know not "seems."

'Tis not alone my inky cloak, good mother,

Nor customary suits of solemn black,

Nor windy suspiration of forced breath,

80   No, nor the fruitful river in the eye,

Nor the dejected havior of the visage,

Together with all forms, moods, shapes of grief,

That can denote me truly. These indeed "seem,"

For they are actions that a man might play;

85   But I have that within which passes⁴⁰ show,

These but the trappings and the suits of woe.

King. 'Tis sweet and commendable in your nature, Hamlet,

To give these mourning duties to your father.

But you must know your father lost a father,

90   That father lost, lost his, and the survivor bound

In filial obligation for some term

To do obsequious sorrow. But to persever

In obstinate condolement is a course

Of impious stubbornness. 'Tis unmanly grief.

---

⁴⁰**passes:** goes beyond.

12. ◀ **REREAD** Reread lines 76–86. According to Hamlet, how does his behavior reflect his innermost feelings? Cite textual evidence in your response.

_____

_____

_____

13. **READ** ▷ As you read lines 87–128, continue to cite textual evidence.

• Underline the feelings Claudius claims to have for Hamlet.

• In the margin, compare the King's words to Hamlet with the Queen's earlier speech to Hamlet.

95   It shows a will most incorrect to heaven,

    A heart unfortified, a mind impatient,

    An understanding simple and unschooled.

    For what we know must be and is as common

    As any the most vulgar thing to sense,

100   Why should we in our **peevish** opposition   **peevish:**

    Take it to heart? Fie, 'tis a fault to heaven,

    A fault against the dead, a fault to nature,

    To reason most absurd, whose common theme

    Is death of fathers, and who still hath cried,

105   From the first corse[41] till he that died today,

    "This must be so." We pray you, throw to earth

    This unprevailing woe and think of us

    As of a father; for let the world take note,

    You are the most immediate to our throne,

110   And with no less nobility of love

    Than that which dearest father bears his son

    Do I impart toward you. For your intent

    In going back to school in Wittenberg,

    It is most retrograde to our desire,

115   And we beseech you, bend you to remain

    Here in the cheer and comfort of our eye,

    Our chiefest courtier, cousin, and our son.

    Queen. Let not thy mother lose her prayers, Hamlet.

    I pray thee, stay with us. Go not to Wittenberg.

120   **Hamlet.** I shall in all my best obey you, madam.

    King. Why, 'tis a loving and a fair reply.

    Be as ourself in Denmark.—Madam, come.

    This gentle and unforced accord of Hamlet

    Sits smiling to my heart, in grace whereof

---

[41] **corse:** corpse.

14. **◀ REREAD** Reread line 120. Why does Hamlet use formal language to cover his feelings? What significance might lie in the fact that he addresses only one person?

_____

_____

_____

125 No jocund health[42] that Denmark drinks today
     But the great cannon to the clouds shall tell,
     And the King's rouse[43] the heaven shall bruit[44] again,
     Respeaking earthly thunder. Come away.
     [*Flourish. All but* Hamlet *exit.*]
     Hamlet. O, that this too, too sullied[45] flesh would melt,
130 Thaw, and resolve itself into a dew,
     Or that the Everlasting had not fixed
     His canon[46] 'gainst self-slaughter! O God, God,
     How weary, stale, flat, and unprofitable
     Seem to me all the uses of this world!
135 Fie on 't, ah fie! 'Tis an unweeded garden
     That grows to seed. Things rank and gross in nature
     Possess it merely.[47] That it should come to this:
     But two months dead—nay, not so much, not two.
     So excellent a king, that was to this
140 Hyperion to a satyr;[48] so loving to my mother
     That he might not beteem[49] the winds of heaven
     Visit her face too roughly. Heaven and earth,
     Must I remember? Why, she would hang on him
     As if increase of appetite had grown
145 By what it fed on. And yet, within a month
     (Let me not think on 't; frailty, thy name is woman!),
     A little month, or ere those shoes were old
     With which she followed my poor father's body,

---

[42]**jocund health:** happy toast.
[43]**rouse:** deep drink.
[44]**bruit:** announce.
[45]**sullied:** stained, defiled.
[46]**canon:** law.
[47]**merely:** entirely.
[48]**Hyperion to a satyr:** In ancient Greek mythology, Hyperion embodied light and wisdom, while a satyr was half man, half goat.
[49]**beteem:** allow.

15. **READal** ▶ As you read lines 129–159, continue to cite textual evidence.

• Underline text that compares the dead King Hamlet and Claudius.

• In the margin, restate the accusations Hamlet makes against Claudius and against his mother.

Like Niobe, all tears—why she, even she

150 (O God, a beast that wants discourse of reason⁵⁰

Would have mourned longer!), married with my uncle,

My father's brother, but no more like my father

Than I to Hercules. Within a month,

Ere yet the salt of most unrighteous tears

155 Had left the flushing in her galled eyes,

She married. O, most wicked speed, to post

With such dexterity to incestuous sheets!

It is not, nor it cannot come to good.

But break, my heart, for I must hold my tongue.

[*Enter* Horatio, Marcellus, *and* Barnardo.]

160 **Horatio.** Hail to your lordship.

Hamlet. I am glad to see you well.

Horatio—or I do forget myself!

Horatio. The same, my lord, and your poor servant ever.

Hamlet. Sir, my good friend. I'll change that name with you.

165 And what make you from⁵¹ Wittenberg, Horatio?—Marcellus?

Marcellus. My good lord.

Hamlet. I am very glad to see you. [*To Barnardo.*]

Good even, sir.—

But what, in faith, make you from Wittenberg?

---

⁵⁰**wants discourse of reason:** lacks the ability to reason.

⁵¹**what make you from:** what are you doing away from.

16. **◀ REREAD** Reread lines 158–159. In what way do these lines sum up the conflict Hamlet feels? Cite textual evidence in your response.

_____

_____

_____

_____

17. **READ ▶** As you read lines 160–196, continue to cite textual evidence.

• Underline an example of Hamlet's use of sarcasm.

• In the margin, tell what Hamlet is bitter about that makes him utter such a sarcastic response.

• Circle the lines that show a change in Hamlet's demeanor. In the margin, explain what news seems to bring new life to him.

> ❝*He was a man. Take him for all in all, I shall not look upon his like again.*❞

170 **Horatio.** A truant disposition, good my lord.

Hamlet. I would not hear your enemy say so,
Nor shall you do my ear that violence
To make it truster of your own report
Against yourself. I know you are no truant.

175 But what is your affair in Elsinore?
We'll teach you to drink deep ere you depart.

Horatio. My lord, I came to see your father's funeral.

Hamlet. I prithee, do not mock me, fellow student.
I think it was to see my mother's wedding.

180 **Horatio.** Indeed, my lord, it followed hard upon.

Hamlet. Thrift, thrift, Horatio. The funeral baked meats
Did coldly furnish forth the marriage tables.
Would I had met my dearest foe in heaven
Or ever I had seen that day, Horatio!

185 My father—methinks I see my father.

Horatio. Where, my lord?

Hamlet.   In my mind's eye, Horatio.

---

18. ◀ **REREAD AND DISCUSS** Reread lines 161–176. In a small group, discuss Hamlet's state of mind. What words would you use to describe his behavior and his reactions to the situation he finds himself in? Explain whether you think his response to this situation is understandable. Cite explicit evidence from the text in your discussion.

Horatio. I saw him once. He was a goodly king.

Hamlet. He was a man. Take him for all in all,

I shall not look upon his like again.

190   **Horatio.** My lord, I think I saw him yesternight.

Hamlet. Saw who?

Horatio. My lord, the King your father.

Hamlet.   The King my father?

Horatio. Season your admiration for a while

With an attent ear, till I may deliver

195   Upon the witness of these gentlemen

This marvel to you.

Hamlet.   For God's love, let me hear!

Horatio. Two nights together had these gentlemen,

Marcellus and Barnardo, on their watch,

In the dead waste and middle of the night,

200   Been thus encountered: a figure like your father,

Armèd at point exactly, cap-à-pie,[52]

Appears before them and with solemn march

Goes slow and stately by them. Thrice he walked

By their oppressed and fear-surprisèd eyes

205   Within his truncheon's length, whilst they, distilled

Almost to jelly with the act of fear,

Stand dumb and speak not to him. This to me

In dreadful secrecy impart they did,

And I with them the third night kept the watch,

210   Where, as they had delivered, both in time,

Form of the thing (each word made true and good),

The apparition comes. I knew your father;

These hands are not more like.

---

[52]**cap-à-pie:** head to foot.

---

19. **READnbsp;▶** As you read lines 197–258, continue to cite textual evidence.

- Circle words that convey feelings of fear.
- Underline text that shows Horatio's assurance that the event took place.
- In the margin, explain how Hamlet's reaction and questions show what kind of a thinker he is.

Hamlet.   But where was this?

Marcellus. My lord, upon the platform where we watch.

215   **Hamlet.** Did you not speak to it?

Horatio.   My lord, I did,

But answer made it none. Yet once methought

It lifted up its head and did address

Itself to motion, like as it would speak;

But even then the morning cock crew loud,

220   And at the sound it shrunk in haste away

And vanished from our sight.

Hamlet.   'Tis very strange.

Horatio. As I do live, my honored lord, 'tis true.

And we did think it writ down in our duty

To let you know of it.

225   **Hamlet.** Indeed, sirs, but this troubles me.

Hold you the watch tonight?

All.   We do, my lord.

Hamlet. Armed, say you?

All.   Armed, my lord.

Hamlet.   From top to toe?

All. My lord, from head to foot.

Hamlet. Then saw you not his face?

230   **Horatio.** O, yes, my lord, he wore his beaver[53] up.

Hamlet. What, looked he frowningly?

Horatio. A countenance more in sorrow than in anger.

Hamlet. Pale or red?

Horatio. Nay, very pale.

Hamlet.   And fixed his eyes upon you?

235   **Horatio.** Most constantly.

Hamlet.   I would I had been there.

Horatio. It would have much amazed you.

Hamlet. Very like. Stayed it long?

Horatio. While one with moderate haste might tell[54] a hundred.

Barnardo/Marcelius. Longer, longer.

240   **Horatio.** Not when I saw 't.

Hamlet.   His beard was grizzled, no?

---

[53]**beaver:** the movable front piece of a helmet.

[54]**tell:** count to.

72

> ## My father's spirit— in arms! All is not well.

Horatio. It was as I have seen it in his life,
A sable silvered.
Hamlet.   I will watch tonight.
Perchance 'twill walk again.
Horatio.   I warrant it will.
Hamlet. If it assume my noble father's person,
245   I'll speak to it, though hell itself should gape
And bid me hold my peace. I pray you all,
If you have hitherto concealed this sight,
Let it be **tenable** in your silence still;
And whatsomever else shall hap tonight,
250   Give it an understanding but no tongue.
I will requite your loves. So fare you well.
Upon the platform, 'twixt eleven and twelve,
I'll visit you.
All.   Our duty to your Honor.
Hamlet. Your loves, as mine to you. Farewell.
[*All but* Hamlet *exit.*]
255   My father's spirit—in arms! All is not well.
I doubt[55] some foul play. Would the night were come!
Till then, sit still, my soul. Foul deeds will rise,
Though all the earth o'erwhelm them, to men's eyes.
[*He exits.*]

tenable:

---

[55] **doubt:** suspect.

20. **◄ REREAD** Reread lines 213–258. What details does Hamlet want to
know about his father's ghost? Why does he find the answers convincing?
Support your response with explicit textual evidence.

_____

_____

_____

_____

_____

_____

SHORT RESPONSE

Cite Text Evidence   Who is Hamlet? What have you learned about him so far?
Explain the person Hamlet appears to be at this point in the play. **Cite text evidence**
to support your response.

_____

_____

_____

_____

_____

_____

_____

_____

_____

Background **Background** Wangari Maathai *(1940–2011) was born in Nyeri, Kenya, in the foothills of Mount Kenya. As a child, she was a star pupil, winning a scholarship in high school to study biology in the United States. Later, she obtained a doctorate from the University of Nairobi, in Kenya, becoming the first woman in East or Central Africa to earn this degree. A friend said of Maathai, "She blazed a trail in whatever she did." She was an environmental activist and, in 1977, began the Green Belt Movement. Its mission was to reforest Kenya, creating jobs for women by having them plant trees. In 2004, she won the Nobel Peace Prize. Below is her acceptance speech.*

Nobel Peace Prize Acceptance Speech

Speech by Wangari Maathai

CLOSE READ
Notes

1. **READ ▷** As you read lines 6–21, begin to cite text evidence.

- Circle the people Maathai is addressing.
- Underline what she says about women and girls.
- In the margin, make an inference about her involvement in women's rights.
- Underline the metaphor she makes about seeds in lines 15–21.

Your Majesties

Your Royal Highnesses

Honourable Members of the Norwegian Nobel Committee

Excellencies

Ladies and Gentlemen

I stand before you and the world humbled by this recognition and uplifted by the honour of being the 2004 Nobel Peace Laureate.

As the first African woman to receive this prize, I accept it on behalf of the people of Kenya and Africa, and indeed the world. I am especially mindful of
10 women and the girl child. I hope it will encourage them to raise their voices and take more space for leadership. I know the honour also gives a deep sense of pride to our men, both old and young. As a mother, I appreciate the inspiration this brings to the youth and urge them to use it to pursue their dreams.

Although this prize comes to me, it acknowledges the work of countless individuals and groups across the globe. They work quietly and often without

recognition to protect the environment, promote democracy, defend human rights and ensure equality between women and men. By so doing, they plant seeds of peace. I know they, too, are proud today. To all who feel represented by

20   this prize I say use it to advance your mission and meet the high expectations the world will place on us.

This honour is also for my family, friends, partners and supporters throughout the world. All of them helped shape the vision and sustain our work, which was often accomplished under hostile conditions. I am also grateful to the people of Kenya—who remained stubbornly hopeful that democracy could be realized and their environment managed sustainably. Because of this support, I am here today to accept this great honour.

I am immensely privileged to join my fellow African Peace laureates, Presidents Nelson Mandela and F.W. de Klerk, Archbishop Desmond Tutu, the

30   late Chief Albert Luthuli, the late Anwar el-Sadat and the UN Secretary General, Kofi Annan.

I know that African people everywhere are encouraged by this news. My fellow Africans, as we embrace this recognition, let us use it to intensify our commitment to our people, to reduce conflicts and poverty and thereby improve their quality of life. Let us embrace democratic governance, protect human rights and protect our environment. I am confident that we shall rise to the occasion. I have always believed that solutions to most of our problems must come from us.

In this year's prize, the Norwegian Nobel Committee has placed the

40   critical issue of environment and its linkage to democracy and peace before the

2.   ◀ **REREAD**   Reread lines 15–21. What main idea is Maathai making in these lines?

_____

_____

3.   **READ** ▶   As you read lines 22–44, continue to cite evidence.

- Circle the statement Maathai makes about the ways in which the Nobel Peace Prize can benefit Africans.
- Underline text describing the link between environment, democracy, and peace.

world. For their visionary action, I am profoundly grateful. Recognizing that
sustainable development,[1] democracy and peace are indivisible is an idea whose
time has come. Our work over the past 30 years has always appreciated and
engaged these linkages.

My inspiration partly comes from my childhood experiences and
observations of Nature in rural Kenya. It has been influenced and nurtured by
the formal education I was privileged to receive in Kenya, the United States and
Germany. As I was growing up, I witnessed forests being cleared and replaced
by commercial plantations, which destroyed local biodiversity[2] and the capacity

50 of the forests to conserve water.

Excellencies, ladies and gentlemen,

In 1977, when we started the Green Belt Movement, I was partly
responding to needs identified by rural women, namely lack of firewood, clean
drinking water, balanced diets, shelter and income.

Throughout Africa, women are the primary caretakers, holding significant
responsibility for tilling the land and feeding their families. As a result, they
are often the first to become aware of environmental damage as resources
become scarce and incapable of sustaining their families.

The women we worked with recounted that unlike in the past, they were

60 unable to meet their basic needs. This was due to the **degradation** of their   degradation:
immediate environment as well as the introduction of commercial farming,
which replaced the growing of household food crops. But international trade
controlled the price of the exports from these small-scale farmers and a
reasonable and just income could not be guaranteed. I came to understand that
when the environment is destroyed, plundered or mismanaged, we undermine
our quality of life and that of future generations.

---

[1] **sustainable development:** construction or development of an area that can be
    maintained over a period of time without damaging the environment.
[2] **biodiversity:** the number and variety of organisms found within a specified geographic
    region.

4. **READ ▷** As you read lines 45–66, continue to cite text evidence.

   • Circle text describing what Maathai witnessed as a young girl growing up in
     Kenya.
   • Underline text describing her reasons for starting the Green Belt Movement.
   • Underline text describing a realization Maathai comes to.

5. **◁ REREAD** Reread lines 55–66. What problems did the women Maathai
   worked with face?

Tree planting became a natural choice to address some of the initial basic needs identified by women. Also, tree planting is simple, attainable and guarantees quick, successful results within a reasonable amount time. This

70 sustains interest and commitment.

So, together, we have planted over 30 million trees that provide fuel, food, shelter, and income to support their children's education and household needs. The activity also creates employment and improves soils and watersheds. Through their involvement, women gain some degree of power over their lives, especially their social and economic position and relevance in the family. This work continues.

Initially, the work was difficult because historically our people have been persuaded to believe that because they are poor, they lack not only capital, but also knowledge and skills to address their challenges. Instead they are

80 conditioned to believe that solutions to their problems must come from 'outside.' Further, women did not realize that meeting their needs depended on their environment being healthy and well managed. They were also unaware

6. **READ ▷** As you read lines 67–76, underline the reasons why tree planting "became a natural choice."

7. **◁ REREAD** Reread lines 67–76. In your own words, explain Matthai's solution to the environmental destruction in her native Kenya. What other needs does her solution meet?

_____

_____

_____

_____

_____

_____

_____

that a degraded environment leads to a scramble for scarce resources and may culminate in poverty and even conflict. They were also unaware of the injustices of international economic arrangements.

In order to assist communities to understand these linkages, we developed a citizen education program, during which people identify their problems, the causes and possible solutions. They then make connections between their own personal actions and the problems they witness in the environment and in society. They learn that our world is confronted with a litany of woes: corruption, violence against women and children, disruption and breakdown of families, and disintegration of cultures and communities. They also identify the abuse of drugs and chemical substances, especially among young people. There are also devastating diseases that are defying cures or occurring in epidemic proportions. Of particular concern are HIV/AIDS, malaria and diseases associated with malnutrition.

On the environment front, they are exposed to many human activities that are devastating to the environment and societies. These include widespread destruction of ecosystems,[3] especially through deforestation,[4] climatic instability, and contamination in the soils and waters that all contribute to excruciating poverty.

---

[3] **ecosystem:** all the living things that share and interact in an environment.
[4] **deforestation:** the cutting down of trees in a large area.

8. **READ ▷** As you read lines 77–109, continue to cite text evidence.

- Circle the problem presented.
- Underline the solution Maathai proposes.
- In the margin, explain the problem and solution described in these lines.

9. **◁ REREAD** Reread lines 86–96. Do you think it's important that people "make connections between their own personal actions and the problems they witness?" Explain.

_____

_____

_____

_____

" *Therefore, the tree became a symbol for the democratic struggle in Kenya.* "

inertia:

In the process, the participants discover that they must be part of the solutions. They realize their hidden potential and are empowered to overcome **inertia** and take action. They come to recognize that they are the primary custodians and beneficiaries of the environment that sustains them.

Entire communities also come to understand that while it is necessary to hold their governments accountable, it is equally important that in their own relationships with each other, they exemplify the leadership values they wish to see in their own leaders, namely justice, integrity and trust.

110   Although initially the Green Belt Movement's tree planting activities did not address issues of democracy and peace, it soon became clear that responsible governance of the environment was impossible without democratic space. Therefore, the tree became a symbol for the democratic struggle in Kenya. Citizens were mobilised to challenge widespread abuses of power, corruption and environmental mismanagement. In Nairobi's Uhuru Park, at Freedom Corner, and in many parts of the country, trees of peace were planted to demand the release of prisoners of conscience and a peaceful transition to democracy.

120   Through the Green Belt Movement, thousands of ordinary citizens were mobilized and empowered to take action and effect change. They learned to overcome fear and a sense of helplessness and moved to defend democratic rights.

In time, the tree also became a symbol for peace and conflict resolution, especially during ethnic conflicts in Kenya when the Green Belt Movement used peace trees to reconcile disputing communities. During the ongoing re-writing of the Kenyan constitution, similar trees of peace were planted in many parts of the country to promote a culture of peace. Using trees as a

10. **READ** ▶ As you read lines 110–148, continue to cite text evidence.

- Underline details that continue to develop the connection between the environment, democracy, and peace.
- In the margin, explain the connection among these ideas.

symbol of peace is in keeping with a widespread African tradition. For example, the elders of the Kikuyu carried a staff from the *thigi* tree that, when placed between two disputing sides, caused them to stop fighting and seek reconciliation. Many communities in Africa have these traditions.

Such practises are part of an extensive cultural heritage, which contributes both to the conservation of habitats and to cultures of peace. With the destruction of these cultures and the introduction of new values, local biodiversity is no longer valued or protected and as a result, it is quickly degraded and disappears. For this reason, The Green Belt Movement explores the concept of cultural biodiversity, especially with respect to indigenous seeds and medicinal plants.

As we progressively understood the causes of environmental degradation, we saw the need for good governance. Indeed, the state of any country's environment is a reflection of the kind of governance in place, and without good governance there can be no peace. Many countries, which have poor governance systems, are also likely to have conflicts and poor laws protecting the environment.

In 2002, the courage, resilience, patience and commitment of members of the Green Belt Movement, other civil society organizations, and the Kenyan public culminated in the peaceful transition to a democratic government and laid the foundation for a more stable society.

11. **◄ REREAD** Reread lines 110–148. Analyze the sequence of events that led from the tree planting of the Green Belt Movement to Kenya's transition to a stable, democratic society. How does the symbolic "tree of peace" connect these events?

_____

_____

_____

_____

_____

_____

_____

This water tank in Kenya was filled the night before, but the water level is now below the spigot. It will not be filled for another week.

Excellencies, friends, ladies and gentlemen,

150   It is 30 years since we started this work. Activities that devastate the environment and societies continue unabated. Today we are faced with a challenge that calls for a shift in our thinking, so that humanity stops threatening its life-support system. We are called to assist the Earth to heal her wounds and in the process heal our own—indeed, to embrace the whole creation in all its diversity, beauty and wonder. This will happen if we see the need to revive our sense of belonging to a larger family of life, with which we have shared our evolutionary process.

consciousness:

In the course of history, there comes a time when humanity is called to shift to a new level of **consciousness**, to reach a higher moral ground. A time

160   when we have to shed our fear and give hope to each other.

That time is now.

The Norwegian Nobel Committee has challenged the world to broaden the understanding of peace: there can be no peace without equitable development; and there can be no development without sustainable management of the environment in a democratic and peaceful space. This shift is an idea whose time has come.

I call on leaders, especially from Africa, to expand democratic space and build fair and just societies that allow the creativity and energy of their citizens to flourish.

12. **READ** ▷ Read lines 149–216. In the margin, explain what Maathai asks of her audience (lines 170–198). Continue to cite text evidence.

170   Those of us who have been privileged to receive education, skills, and experiences and even power must be role models for the next generation of leadership. In this regard, I would also like to appeal for the freedom of my fellow laureate Aung San Suu Kyi[5] so that she can continue her work for peace and democracy for the people of Burma and the world at large.

Culture plays a central role in the political, economic and social life of communities. Indeed, culture may be the missing link in the development of Africa. Culture is dynamic and evolves over time, consciously discarding retrogressive traditions, like female genital mutilation (FGM), and embracing aspects that are good and useful.

180   Africans, especially, should re-discover positive aspects of their culture. In accepting them, they would give themselves a sense of belonging, identity and self-confidence.

Ladies and Gentlemen,

There is also need to galvanize civil society and grassroots movements to catalyse change. I call upon governments to recognize the role of these social movements in building a critical mass of responsible citizens, who help maintain checks and balances in society. On their part, civil society should embrace not only their rights but also their responsibilities.

Further, industry and global institutions must appreciate that ensuring
190   economic justice, equity and ecological integrity are of greater value than profits at any cost.

The extreme global inequities and prevailing consumption patterns continue at the expense of the environment and peaceful co-existence. The choice is ours.

I would like to call on young people to commit themselves to activities that contribute toward achieving their long-term dreams. They have the energy and creativity to shape a sustainable future. To the young people I say, you are a gift to your communities and indeed the world. You are our hope and our future.

The holistic approach to development, as exemplified by the Green Belt
200   Movement, could be embraced and replicated in more parts of Africa and beyond. It is for this reason that I have established the Wangari Maathai Foundation to ensure the continuation and expansion of these activities. Although a lot has been achieved, much remains to be done.

Excellencies, ladies and gentlemen,

As I conclude I reflect on my childhood experience when I would visit a stream next to our home to fetch water for my mother. I would drink water

---

[5] **Aung San Suu Kyi:** Burmese political leader who had been under house arrest for 15 years for espousing human rights; she was awarded the Nobel Peace Prize in 1991 and was freed in 2010.

straight from the stream. Playing among the arrowroot leaves I tried in vain to pick up the strands of frogs' eggs, believing they were beads. But every time I put my little fingers under them they would break. Later, I saw thousands of

210   tadpoles: black, energetic and wriggling through the clear water against the background of the brown earth. This is the world I inherited from my parents.

Today, over 50 years later, the stream has dried up, women walk long distances for water, which is not always clean, and children will never know what they have lost. The challenge is to restore the home of the tadpoles and give back to our children a world of beauty and wonder.

Thank you very much.

13.   ◀ REREAD   Reread lines 205–216. Explain in the margin why Maathai ends with this story of her childhood.

SHORT RESPONSE

Cite Text Evidence   Analyze Maathai's ideas that explain how the environment, democracy, and peace interact and are interconnected. Review your reading notes to trace the development of these ideas over the course of the speech, and **cite text evidence** in your response.

_____

_____

_____

_____

_____

_____

_____

_____

_____

_____

Taking Risks

Taking Risks

"It is only by risking our persons from one hour to another that we live at all."

—William James

Background *The name of the English poet who created* Beowulf *is lost to history. The narrative probably originated on the European continent around the sixth century. Versions were carried to England by emigrating Germanic tribespeople and were passed down orally. Sometime in the eighth century, the story was probably shaped by a single unknown writer into the form in which it is known today.* Beowulf *is a powerful warrior of the Geats, a people from what is now Sweden. He is known for his bravery and his almost superhuman strength. In his youth, he killed a vicious monster known as Grendel and later his equally terrifying mother.*

from Beowulf

Epic Poem by The Beowulf Poet   translated by Burton Raffel

1. **READU** ▷ As you read lines 1–27, begin to collect and cite text evidence.

   - Underline courageous deeds Beowulf has done and what he promises to do.
   - In the margin, explain what you can infer about Beowulf (lines 1–6 and lines 20–27).

Beowulf's Last Battle

Beowulf is now king of the Geats and has ruled in peace and prosperity for fifty years. One day, a fire-breathing dragon begins terrorizing the Geats. Beowulf, now an old man, takes on the challenge of fighting it. He goes to the dragon's den with a hand-picked group of warriors.

And Beowulf uttered his final boast:[1]
"I've never known fear, as a youth I fought
In endless battles. I am old, now,
But I will fight again, seek fame still,
5   If the dragon hiding in his tower dares
To face me."

---
[1] **boast:** a ritualized statement that is both a recitation of prior deeds and a vow to meet an approaching challenge.

Then he said farewell to his followers,

Each in his turn, for the last time:

"I'd use no sword, no weapon, if this beast

Could be killed without it, crushed to death

10   Like Grendel, gripped in my hands and torn

Limb from limb. But his breath will be burning

Hot, poison will pour from his tongue.

I feel no shame, with shield and sword

And armor, against this monster: when he comes to me

15   I mean to stand, not run from his shooting

Flames, stand till fate decides

Which of us wins. My heart is firm,

My hands calm: I need no hot

Words. Wait for me close by, my friends.

20   We shall see, soon, who will survive

This bloody battle, stand when the fighting

Is done. No one else could do

What I mean to, here, no man but me

Could hope to defeat this monster. No one

25   Could try. And this dragon's treasure, his gold

And everything hidden in that tower, will be mine

Or war will sweep me to a bitter death!"

Then Beowulf rose, still brave, still strong,

And with his shield at his side, and a mail shirt on his breast,

---

2. ◀ **REREAD** Reread lines 1–6. When Beowulf talks about himself, which
traits is he proudest of? Support your answer with explicit textual evidence.

_____

_____

_____

_____

3. **READ** ▶ As you read lines 28–81, continue to cite textual evidence.

• Underline text that describes the setting.

• Circle text that shows the turning point in the battle.

• In the margin, explain how the details of the setting create tension (lines
  36–55).

30 Strode calmly, confidently, toward the tower, under

The rocky cliffs: no coward could have walked there!

And then he who'd endured dozens of desperate

Battles, who'd stood boldly while swords and shields

Clashed, the best of kings, saw

35 Huge stone arches and felt the heat

Of the dragon's breath, flooding down

Through the hidden entrance, too hot for anyone

To stand, a streaming current of fire

And smoke that blocked all passage. And the Geats'

40 Lord and leader, angry, lowered

His sword and roared out a battle cry,

A call so loud and clear that it reached through

The **hoary** rock, hung in the dragon's

Ear. The beast rose, angry,

45 Knowing a man had come—and then nothing

But war could have followed. Its breath came first,

A steaming cloud pouring from the stone,

Then the earth itself shook. Beowulf

Swung his shield into place, held it

50 In front of him, facing the entrance. The dragon

Coiled and uncoiled, its heart urging it

Into battle. Beowulf's ancient sword

Was waiting, unsheathed, his sharp and gleaming

Blade. The beast came closer; both of them

55 Were ready, each set on slaughter. The Geats'

Great prince stood firm, unmoving, prepared

Behind his high shield, waiting in his shining

Armor. The monster came quickly toward him,

Pouring out fire and smoke, hurrying

60 To its fate. Flames beat at the iron

Shield, and for a time it held, protected

hoary:

4. **◀ REREAD** Reread lines 45–58. How does the poet show that the dragon is similar to Beowulf? What are those similarities? Support your answer with explicit textual evidence.

_____

_____

_____

CLOSE READ
Notes

89

Beowulf as he'd planned; then it began to melt,

And for the first time in his life that famous prince

Fought with fate against him, with glory

65 Denied him. He knew it, but he raised his sword

And struck at the dragon's scaly hide.

The ancient blade broke, bit into

The monster's skin, drew blood, but cracked

And failed him before it went deep enough, helped him

70 Less than he needed. The dragon leaped

With pain, thrashed and beat at him, spouting

Murderous flames, spreading them everywhere.

And the Geats' ring-giver[2] did not boast of glorious

Victories in other wars: his weapon

75 Had failed him, deserted him, now when he needed it

Most, that excellent sword. Edgetho's[3]

Famous son stared at death,

Unwilling to leave this world, to exchange it

For a dwelling in some distant place—a journey

80 Into darkness that all men must make, as death

Ends their few brief hours on earth.

Quickly, the dragon came at him, encouraged

As Beowulf fell back; its breath flared,

And he suffered, wrapped around in swirling

85 Flames—a king, before, but now

A beaten warrior. None of his comrades

Came to him, helped him, his brave and noble

Followers; they ran for their lives, fled

Deep in a wood. And only one of them

90 Remained, stood there, miserable, remembering,

As a good man must, what kinship should mean.

His name was Wiglaf, he was Wexstan's son

And a good soldier; his family had been Swedish,

Once. Watching Beowulf, he could see

---

[2] **ring-giver:** king, lord; When someone swore allegiance to a Germanic lord in return for protection, the lord typically bestowed a ring on the follower to symbolize the bond.

[3] **Edgetho:** Beowulf's father.

---

5. **READ** ▶ As you read lines 82–130, continue to cite textual evidence.

- Underline text explaining what Wiglaf and his comrades promised in the past and what Wiglaf wants them to do now.

- In the margin, explain the irony of the narrator's words in lines 82–91.

95 How his king was suffering, burning. Remembering

Everything his lord and cousin had given him,

Armor and gold and the great estates

Wexstan's family enjoyed, Wiglaf's

Mind was made up; he raised his yellow

100 Shield and drew his sword. . . .

       And Wiglaf, his heart heavy, uttered

The kind of words his comrades deserved:

      "I remember how we sat in the mead-hall, drinking

And boasting of how brave we'd be when Beowulf

105 Needed us, he who gave us these swords

And armor: all of us swore to repay him,

When the time came, kindness for kindness

—With our lives, if he needed them. He allowed us to join him,

Chose us from all his great army, thinking

110 Our boasting words had some weight, believing

Our promises, trusting our swords. He took us

For soldiers, for men. He meant to kill

This monster himself, our mighty king,

Fight this battle alone and unaided,

115 As in the days when his strength and daring dazzled

Men's eyes. But those days are over and gone

And now our lord must lean on younger

Arms. And we must go to him, while angry

Flames burn at his flesh, help

120 Our glorious king! By almighty God,

I'd rather burn myself than see

Flames swirling around my lord.

And who are we to carry home

Our shields before we've slain his enemy

125 And ours, to run back to our homes with Beowulf

So hard-pressed here? I swear that nothing

He ever did deserved an end

Like this, dying miserably and alone,

Butchered by this savage beast: we swore

130 That these swords and armor were each for us all!" . . .

6. ◀ REREAD AND DISCUSS Reread lines 92–130. In a small group, discuss
the details Wiglaf gives that depict Beowulf as an honorable king. How does
Wiglaf show his own honor?

7. **READ** ▶ As you read lines 131–189, continue to collect and cite textual evidence.

- Underline text that shows Beowulf's awareness of his approaching death and how he faces it.
- In the margin, explain why Beowulf's statement in lines 137–140 is important for the Geats.

The Death of Beowulf

Wiglaf joins Beowulf, who again attacks the dragon single-handedly; but the remnant of Beowulf's sword shatters, and the monster wounds him in the neck. Wiglaf then strikes the dragon, and he and Beowulf together finally succeed in killing the beast. Their triumph is short-lived, however, because Beowulf's wound proves to be mortal.

livid:

Beowulf spoke, in spite of the swollen,
Livid wound, knowing he'd unwound
His string of days on earth, seen
As much as God would grant him; all worldly
135 Pleasure was gone, as life would go,
Soon:
 "I'd leave my armor to my son,
Now, if God had given me an heir,
A child born of my body, his life
Created from mine. I've worn this crown
140 For fifty winters: no neighboring people
Have tried to threaten the Geats, sent soldiers
Against us or talked of terror. My days
Have gone by as fate willed, waiting
For its word to be spoken, ruling as well
145 As I knew how, swearing no unholy oaths,
Seeking no lying wars. I can leave
This life happy; I can die, here,
Knowing the Lord of all life has never
Watched me wash my sword in blood
150 Born of my own family. Belovèd
Wiglaf, go, quickly, find
The dragon's treasure: we've taken its life,
But its gold is ours, too. Hurry,

Bring me ancient silver, precious

155   Jewels, shining armor and gems,

Before I die. Death will be softer,

Leaving life and this people I've ruled

So long, if I look at this last of all prizes."

       Then Wexstan's son went in, as quickly

160   As he could, did as the dying Beowulf

Asked, entered the inner darkness

Of the tower, went with his mail shirt and his sword.

Flushed with victory he groped his way,

A brave young warrior, and suddenly saw

165   Piles of gleaming gold, precious

Gems, scattered on the floor, cups

And bracelets, rusty old helmets, beautifully

Made but rotting with no hands to rub

And polish them. They lay where the dragon left them;

170   It had flown in the darkness, once, before fighting

Its final battle. (So gold can easily

Triumph, defeat the strongest of men,

No matter how deep it is hidden!) And he saw,

Hanging high above, a golden

175   Banner, woven by the best of weavers

And beautiful. And over everything he saw

A strange light, shining everywhere,

On walls and floor and treasure. Nothing

Moved, no other monsters appeared;

180   He took what he wanted, all the treasures

That pleased his eye, heavy plates

8.   ◀ REREAD   Reread lines 139–150. How does Beowulf summarize his 50-year reign? What ideals are reflected in his speech? Support your answer with explicit textual evidence.

_____

_____

_____

_____

_____

And golden cups and the glorious banner,

Loaded his arms with all they could hold.

Beowulf's dagger, his iron blade,

185   Had finished the fire-spitting terror

That once protected tower and treasures

Alike; the gray-bearded lord of the Geats

Had ended those flying, burning raids

Forever.

            Then Wiglaf went back, anxious

190   To return while Beowulf was alive, to bring him

Treasure they'd won together. He ran,

Hoping his wounded king, weak

And dying, had not left the world too soon.

Then he brought their treasure to Beowulf, and found

195   His famous king bloody, gasping

For breath. But Wiglaf sprinkled water

Over his lord, until the words

Deep in his breast broke through and were heard.

Beholding the treasure he spoke, haltingly:

200   "For this, this gold, these jewels, I thank

Our Father in Heaven, Ruler of the Earth—

For all of this, that His grace has given me,

Allowed me to bring to my people while breath

Still came to my lips. I sold my life

205   For this treasure, and I sold it well. Take

What I leave, Wiglaf, lead my people,

Help them; my time is gone. Have

The brave Geats build me a tomb,

When the funeral flames have burned me, and build it

210   Here, at the water's edge, high

On this spit of land, so sailors can see

This tower, and remember my name, and call it

Beowulf's tower, and boats in the darkness

And mist, crossing the sea, will know it."

9. **READ** ▶ As you read lines 190–226, continue to cite textual evidence.

- Underline text that shows Wiglaf's feelings toward Beowulf.
- Circle text explaining who Beowulf chooses as a successor.
- In the margin, explain how lines 210–218 demonstrate a value important to the Geats.

215   Then that brave king gave the golden

Necklace from around his throat to Wiglaf,

Gave him his gold-covered helmet, and his rings,

And his mail shirt, and ordered him to use them well:

       "You're the last of all our far-flung family.

220 Fate has swept our race away,

Taken warriors in their strength and led them

To the death that was waiting. And now I follow them."

       The old man's mouth was silent, spoke

No more, had said as much as it could;

225 He would sleep in the fire, soon. His soul

Left his flesh, flew to glory. . . .

       And when the battle was over Beowulf's followers

Came out of the wood, cowards and traitors,

Knowing the dragon was dead. Afraid,

230 While it spit its fires, to fight in their lord's

Defense, to throw their **javelins** and spears,

They came like shamefaced jackals, their shields

In their hands, to the place where the prince lay dead,

And waited for Wiglaf to speak. He was sitting

235 Near Beowulf's body, wearily sprinkling

Water in the dead man's face, trying

To stir him. He could not. No one could have kept

javelins:

10. **◀ REREAD**   Reread lines 215–222. What happens in these lines? Why is it important that we have seen Wiglaf's courage in battle as well as his loyalty to Beowulf?

_____

_____

_____

_____

11. **READ ▶**   As you read lines 227–265, continue to cite text evidence.

- Underline examples of kennings (metaphorical compound words substituted for a single noun) that stand for Beowulf's name.

- In the margin, explain how Wiglaf grows into his position as the new leader (lines 245–257).

Life in their lord's body, or turned

Aside the Lord's will: world

240 And men and all move as He orders,

And always have, and always will.

Then Wiglaf turned and angrily told them

What men without courage must hear.

Wexstan's brave son stared at the traitors,

245 His heart sorrowful, and said what he had to:

"I say what anyone who speaks the truth

Must say. . . .

Too few of his warriors remembered

To come, when our lord faced death, alone.

250 And now the giving of swords, of golden

Rings and rich estates, is over,

Ended for you and everyone who shares

Your blood: when the brave Geats hear

How you bolted and ran none of your race

255 Will have anything left but their lives. And death

Would be better for them all, and for you, than the kind

Of life you can lead, branded with disgrace!". . .

Then the warriors rose,

Walked slowly down from the cliff, stared

260 At those wonderful sights, stood weeping as they saw

Beowulf dead on the sand, their bold

Ring-giver resting in his last bed;

He'd reached the end of his days, their mighty

War-king, the great lord of the Geats,

265 Gone to a glorious death. . . .

---

12. ◀ REREAD Reread lines 245–260. How does this passage demonstrate
the importance of loyalty and bravery for the Geats?

_____

_____

_____

_____

_____

_____

13. **READ ▷** As you read lines 266–292, continue to collect and cite textual evidence.

- Underline text describing how the Geats mourned for Beowulf.
- In the margin, explain what the use of the word *beloved* reveals about the relationship between a leader and his people in the time of the Geats.

Mourning Beowulf

After Beowulf dies, the Geats fulfill his wish to build a tower as his tomb. The tower and the warriors' actions after building it serve to broadcast Beowulf's legacy not just to the Geats themselves but to others beyond the lands where Beowulf ruled.

      Then the Geats built the tower, as Beowulf
Had asked, strong and tall, so sailors
Could find it from far and wide; working
For ten long days they made his monument,
270 Sealed his ashes in walls as straight
And high as wise and willing hands
Could raise them. And the riches he and Wiglaf
Had won from the dragon, rings, necklaces,
Ancient, hammered armor—all
275 The treasures they'd taken were left there, too,
Silver and jewels buried in the sandy
Ground, back in the earth, again
And forever hidden and useless to men.
And then twelve of the bravest Geats
280 Rode their horses around the tower,
Telling their sorrow, telling stories
Of their dead king and his greatness, his glory,
Praising him for heroic deeds, for a life
As noble as his name. So should all men
285 Raise up words for their lords, warm
With love, when their shield and protector leaves
His body behind, sends his soul
On high. And so Beowulf's followers
Rode, mourning their belovèd leader,
290 Crying that no better king had ever
Lived, no prince so mild, no man
So open to his people, so deserving of praise.

14. **◄ REREAD** Reread lines 282–286. Notice the alliteration in the phrases "words for their lords" and "warm with love." How would you describe the tone of these lines? Cite another example of alliteration in your response.

_____

_____

_____

_____

SHORT RESPONSE

Cite Text Evidence   What traits make Beowulf an epic hero? Support your answer by **citing explicit textual evidence.**

_____

_____

_____

_____

_____

_____

_____

_____

_____

_____

_____

_____

Background **Mark Brazaitis** *was born in Cleveland, Ohio, in 1966. He is the author of five books, including* The Incurables: Stories. *Brazaitis has said, ". . . the place I learned to write was Guatemala, where I was a Peace Corps Volunteer from 1990 to 1993. To step out of one's culture and one's language is to see oneself and one's country and everything one has ever believed in in fresh and even startling ways."*

Blackheart

Short Story by Mark Brazaitis

CLOSE READ
Notes

1. **READD** ▷ As you read lines 1–32, begin to collect and cite text evidence.

- Circle text describing the setting.
- Underline things Emily's mother tells her.
- In the margin, explain why Emily could not stay with her father (lines 5–15) and why she is in Argentina (lines 16–32).

The moon is full, the sky cloudless. It is summer in Argentina—"All your friends in Ohio are shivering in the snow," her mother told her the other day—but the nights are cool. She walks across the garden's lawn toward the door on the other end. It is the door to the vineyard. Black Heart is behind it.

Her mother and Ed are eating dinner in Mendoza. It is late, but dinner always starts late in Argentina. The restaurants open at eight at night. Emily has eaten dinner at a restaurant in Argentina only once, and she fell asleep before dessert. Waking her, her mother said, "You'll never be mistaken for an Argentine." Ed had said the same in relation to her red hair and blue-green

10 eyes, inherited from her father. Emily wanted to stay with her father in Sherman instead of coming here, but he has a new girlfriend and Emily's presence, he said, would be inconvenient now. There was a time between her parents' separation and divorce when her father wanted her to spend all her time with him. Her mother said this was only because he wanted to look good in the eyes of the divorce judge. After the divorce, he became busy.

So did her mother, who met Ed in an adventure writing class he'd taught in Cleveland. Older than her mother by sixteen years, he has a balloon belly and

waddles rather than walks. He is a travel writer, a food writer, a wine writer. He
has rented this house outside of Mendoza so he can write about Mendoza's
20   foods and wines. Her mother is supposed to be home-schooling her—Emily's
fifth-grade teacher gave her mother a packet to cover January and February,
the months they would be gone—but most days, her mother and Ed drive off
into the Uco valley, and Emily leaves her schoolwork and wanders around the
vineyard singing songs she knows and songs she makes up. Beyond the last row
of grapevines, there is an elevated spot, a grass altar where she likes to lie on
her back and stare at the Andes Mountains, off to the west, snow-capped and
shimmering like a picture in a storybook. Sometimes Maria, the wife of the
man who looks after the property, finds her and asks if she's all right. Maria's
Spanish is only a little better than Emily's. Maria and her husband, Daniel, who
30   live in the two-room cottage next to the house where she is staying, are from
Bolivia. Her mother says their first language is . . . Emily can't remember. It
starts with a q, like question.

     Daniel is in charge of keeping the robbers and the killers and the rapists
out of the vineyard and out of the garden and out of the house. One night, she
overheard her mother and Ed discussing what happened to a Canadian woman
who owns a hotel in Mendoza. When her mother discovered her hiding behind
the kitchen door, she said, "You don't have to worry, sweetheart. We have
Daniel and the dogs."

     Their house sits in the north end of the garden, and the garden is
40   surrounded by a black iron fence topped with barbed wire. On three sides of
the black fence, separated from it by a ten-foot-wide corridor, is a chain-link
fence, also topped with barbed wire. On the fourth side of the garden, on the
south end, is the vineyard, which is surrounded by only a five-foot-tall wooden
picket fence without barbed wire. Before Daniel goes to bed, he releases three
bullmastiffs into the corridors between the black fence and the chain-link
fence. Into the vineyard Daniel sends a fourth dog, some combination of pit
bull, Rottweiler, German shepherd, and wolf, an animal as cruel and vicious as
any animal on earth, or so Daniel told her. Daniel has given several names to

2. (◀ REREAD) Reread lines 10–32. In the margin, explain why you think
Maria asks Emily if she's "all right."

3. (READ ▶) As you read lines 33–69, continue to cite textual evidence.

- Underline text describing Black Heart.
- In the margin, make an inference about why Emily is so interested in the dogs
(lines 49–57).

this dog in his language, but in Spanish he calls him Black Heart. Black Heart
50   was the topic of her mother's sternest lecture: *At night, don't ever open the door
to the vineyard. Black Heart is on guard, and he's trained to kill whomever he
finds.* "Even me?" *Anyone. Please, darling.* "Why would he kill me?" *Please.
Never open the door.*

When they arrived in Argentina, Ed thought she should be curious about
wine and empanadas and tango dancing. But Emily was curious about the
guard dogs. How old were they? Were the three bullmastiffs brothers? Had the
three bullmastiffs ever met Black Heart? Had Black Heart ever killed anyone?

Ed didn't know anything about them. "Ask Daniel," he said. So Emily did,
in her bad Spanish. The next time they saw each other, Daniel pulled a tattered
60   paperback Spanish-English dictionary from his back pocket. The print was so
small even Emily had trouble reading it. The dictionary became a game
between them, a game to see who could find the right word, who could speak it
well enough so the other person understood. Daniel is only an inch or two
taller than her five feet (she is the tallest girl in her class), and he has the
blackest, straightest hair she's ever seen. His nose is large, and his nostrils seem,
in proportion, even larger. Her mother and Ed call him Evo, because he
supposedly looks like the president of Bolivia. Saturday is his night off.
Sometimes on Saturday nights he stays home with Maria and sometimes he
meets up with his Bolivian friends in Mendoza.

70   Often when Daniel returns late at night, she hears him singing, and this
reminds her of her father, who loves to sing. Daniel's voice is light and sweet;
her father's is low like a rumble or a growl. When her parents were married, the
three of them would go camping every summer in southern Ohio, and every
night around the fire, her mother would play her guitar and her father would

4. **◀ REREAD** Reread lines 58–69. How does Emily forge a relationship with
Daniel and his dogs? What might this relationship have to do with the
theme of the story?

_____

_____

_____

_____

5. **READ ▶** As you read lines 70–117, continue to cite textual evidence.

• Underline text that mentions Emily's father.
• Make notes in the margin about the appearance and behavior of Black Heart.

enchanting:

sing, his voice booming above the crackling flames. On the last couple of trips, Emily sang with him. Although her voice was as thin as air, it was beautiful, her father said, beautiful and **enchanting**. "You could sing a fish out of the water," he said. "You could sing a dog away from a bone."

80   In the week before she left for Argentina, Emily called her father every day, always when she thought his girlfriend wouldn't be with him. Even when she wasn't, their conversations were short. One time Emily called him and his girlfriend interrupted to ask him, "What do you think of this ring?" The last time she spoke to him, he was at a party and there was music in the background. "Remember this song?" he said, and she sang to show him she did. But she realized he had been speaking to someone else. Embarrassed, she hung up. The next day, she was on a plane to Argentina.

    Emily hears a sound in the bougainvillea that covers the black iron fence on her left. Her heart springs into her throat. But it is only the stray tiger cat who visits some nights. Daniel calls him Romeo because he supposedly

90 fathered all the recent litters in the neighborhood. He paws his way from the

cascades:

top of the fence, **cascades** down the purple flowers, and tumbles onto the grass. He is the thinnest cat she has ever seen, but her mother assured her he isn't starving.

    Romeo rubs himself against her leg, and she crouches down to pet him. His fur is like none she has touched before. It is thick and prickly like she imagines a groundhog's would be. "Do you know what I'm doing tonight?" she asks Romeo. "I'm going to visit Black Heart." He looks up at her, responding to her voice. "Don't worry. He's my friend. I've been visiting him in his cage. I sing to him." She pretends he says something. "He's not my boyfriend! He's a dog!"

100 She laughs and shakes her head.

    In her first week in Argentina, after they had become friends, Daniel brought her to see the dogs in their cages, located in the corridor between the

---

6.   **◀ REREAD**   Reread lines 70–86. Describe how Emily's relationship with her father has changed. Support your answer with explicit textual evidence.

_____

_____

_____

_____

two fences at the front of the property. They were like cages at the zoo, except they were no taller than her chest. The three bullmastiffs, who shared a cage, barked at her, but when Daniel scolded them, they whimpered like doves. When they reached Black Heart's cage, he attacked the bars, barking like no dog she'd ever known, like some creature from mythology. Surprised and frightened, she backpedaled and tripped. Daniel alternately spoke sympathetically to her and harshly to Black Heart. From where she'd fallen, she

110 gazed, trembling, at Black Heart, who never ceased barking. She wondered how strong the bars of his cage were. She imagined them snapping and Black Heart pouncing on her and enclosing her neck in his mouth.

Black Heart looked less like a dog and more like a mammal from the period after the dinosaurs died. He was husky and broad-shouldered like a gorilla and his square face and dark, marble eyes seemed bison-like. He had scars everywhere—on his forehead, on his chest, in several places on his back—and she wondered what violent encounter each scar represented.

Thereafter whenever Daniel fed the dogs she accompanied him—except when her mother was around. Her mother didn't want her near the dogs. "They

120 are not your friends," she said. "Okay, Emily? Okay?"

When she was with Daniel, she stood by his side, so close she could smell him. He wore cologne, but this didn't disguise his other smells, which she thought her mother would find repulsive but which she grew used to and found reassuring. As soon as Daniel fed the three bullmastiffs, which he did by sliding their bowls into a space on the bottom of their cage, they stopped being interested in anything but the food. But Black Heart wouldn't eat his food until Daniel and Emily retreated behind the garden wall. If they craned their heads around the wall to stare at Black Heart, he would start barking like he smelled blood. To watch him eat, Daniel taped a hand-held mirror to a long stick and

130 held it at such an angle that they could gaze into it and see him. He ate the brown nuggets with slow pleasure. She remembered the last time she ate dinner with her father, how he picked at the rotisserie chicken, finishing everything on the bones.

When Daniel lets Black Heart into the vineyard every night, he carries a bullwhip. The whip looks like a snake—*una culebra*—and Black Heart is scared

---

7. **READ ▶** As you read lines 118–172, continue to cite textual evidence.

• Make notes in the margin about Emily's relationship with Black Heart.

• Underline the reference to Emily's father.

• Circle the sentence that describes the danger Black Heart might present.

of nothing in the world except the whip. Even so, he growls at it as if to say, Keep your distance or I will attack you. A week ago, as she leaned out of her open bedroom window, she saw Daniel leading Black Heart into the vineyard.
Under his breath, he said, "One night he won't be afraid of the whip. And then what?" He looked up at her, surprised to see her. She smiled like she did when she didn't understand his Spanish.

"All right, Romeo," she says, "you be good. Be good to all your girlfriends." He darts off to the other side of the garden and disappears beneath the weeping willow tree, which in the night looks like a hunched giant with a thousand thin arms. She resumes her walk toward the door, but is stopped by a sound of "Who? Who? Who?" It is Boy, the white-faced owl, in his nook in the palm tree twenty feet above her. She always thought of owls as old, but this owl looks like a teenager—thus the name she gave him.

"It's only me, Boy," she says. If he could speak in a language she understood, she wonders if he would tease her like a brother would. Or would he say something like the man at the mall said to her cousin, who is fourteen but, with her European haircut, looks twenty?

"I'm going to visit Black Heart," she tells the owl. "It's all right. You'll see."

Some days when Daniel is out in the vineyard and Maria is at the market in Luján de Cuyo and her mother and Ed are napping under the thin-bladed ceiling fan in their bedroom or sampling wines in Chacras de Coria, she visits Black Heart in his cage. She used to bring him pieces of steak and chicken she slipped into her palm at dinner and saved in a paper bag beneath her bed. The first time, she tossed the pieces of meat between the bars of his cage and retreated behind the fence so he could eat them in private. When, on **subsequent** visits, she lingered, he snarled, growled, and barked at her but eventually, between his hostile sounds, devoured her offering.

One day, she sang to him after giving him his meat, and his vicious sounds ceased. Even with his gigantic, square head and his razor-blade teeth and his terrible scars, he looked familiar and approachable, like a misunderstood monster. The song she'd sung was one she'd heard often on Maria's radio. She didn't understand all of the Spanish words, but she could **enunciate** them clearly, and Black Heart cocked his head as if to hear better. As soon as she stopped, his face again became strange and hideous, and his barking shocked her ears until she fled, terrified.

The next day, she returned with only her voice. As long as she sang, he was silent, docile, calm. Content, even. Perhaps even happy.

Boy flutters his white and brown wings and swoops down toward her, his mouth open, his talons spread and pointed like daggers. As she ducks and

140

150

160

170

subsequent:

enunciate:

covers her eyes, she feels the wind from his wings fill her hair. She shivers from fear and a strange pleasure before she hears a squeal, high-pitched and hopeless. She turns to see Boy pluck a mouse from the grass and retreat with his feast to the palm tree.

"You scared me, Boy. Maybe you wanted to? In fun, I mean. Like a brother
180 would?"

The day she touched Black Heart, the air was a white mist. She couldn't see her feet. But she knew the path to his cage as if it were illuminated. When she stood before it, she couldn't see him; she could only hear his terrible bark. When she sang, his barking stopped instantly, as if she'd cast a spell. Piercing the bars of his cage, she held out her hand to him, palm open. She felt his mouth engulf it. She felt his teeth touch her skin. She thought he was going to bite down. But his mouth held steady. Carefully, she slipped her left hand into the cage so she could stroke his head and neck and back. His fur was like the leather of her father's jacket.

190 A moment later, she felt his tongue sweep the underside of her fingers and his teeth nibble, soft as a kiss, her fingertips. She felt her heart fly. She felt adored. For hours afterward, she didn't wash either hand.

During her last visit before tonight, as she sang a song she'd invented about a girl and a dog and the iron between them, he looked at her with what she swore was a plea. *I want to know you without bars between us.*

---

8. **◀ REREAD** Reread lines 163–172. How does Emily's singing affect Black Heart? What might singing have to do with the theme of the story?

_____

_____

_____

_____

_____

9. **READ ▶** As you read lines 173–209, continue to cite textual evidence.

- Underline text describing Emily's reactions to Boy and Black Heart.
- Circle the words that Emily imagines Black Heart speaks.
- In the margin, explain how Emily is testing the limits of her power.

Ten feet from the door separating her and Black Heart, she stops. She can sense his presence. She hears a growl so soft it might be a purr. If she moves any closer, he will erupt and wake Maria, asleep in her tiny house. If this happens, her plan will come to nothing, and she will never again have the chance to visit

200   him. Ed and her mother will keep her with them, even if they'd rather not. Besides, their time in Argentina is coming to an end.

Another week, and they will be heading home.

She sings, softly at first, a sound like small waves hitting sand. He stops growling. She reaches the door. There are three deadbolt locks, the highest an inch beyond her reach. But she jumps and slaps it open. In jumping, her singing stops, and Black Heart growls. She slaps the second lock open, her singing coming jagged, and Black Heart continues to growl, his voice climbing in register the way it does before he attacks the bars of his cage. She tries to make her singing calm, but this is difficult because of her pounding heart.

210   She has one deadbolt left to open before she can turn the doorknob and release him into the garden. She gives herself a moment to doubt. The wisest part of her says she should go back to the house, go to bed. But her hand, which she can barely feel as her heart thunders, acts otherwise. It snaps the deadbolt to the side.

Stop, she tells herself. Think. If Black Heart were to attack her, Maria could do nothing. Daniel is in Mendoza with his friends. He might come home in five minutes. He might come home in three hours. And Ed and her mother? Even if they were to come, what could they do?

---

10. **◀ REREAD** Reread lines 196–202. What is Emily's plan? Why is her relationship with Black Heart important to her? Support your answer with explicit textual evidence.

_____

_____

_____

_____

11. **READ ▶** As you read lines 210–264, continue to cite textual evidence.

- Underline text that describes Emily's excitement and fear.
- Circle verbs and verb phrases that show Black Heart's movements.

These reservations register the way the deepest fear does, like fingers
squeezing her heart, but they cannot overcome her desire. She pulls open the
door. Boy cries as if he's been wounded, leaps from his cave in the palm tree,
and flies over her, his wings filling her hair with a warning wind.

Too late. Black Heart is at her side, so close she can feel heat coming from
him. She thinks, I'm going to die. At the same time, **exhilaration** fills her. She
feels like she owns the night. She turns, singing, and walks to the middle of the
garden. Black Heart circles her, a slow loop on the grass, his eyes never leaving
her. He might be dancing with her. Or he might be a lion circling its prey.

The moon blazes above her, and she feels powerful and magical and
adored. Every so often, she touches Black Heart's back, at once smooth and
rough. *I can sing all night.* But after a minute or five or ten—she has no watch,
the night tells no time—her exhilaration fades into worry. She doesn't know
how long she can stand here and sing. Perhaps she can make her way back to
the house, open the door, slip in. It is only fifty feet from where she's standing.
But when she steps toward it, Black Heart quickly moves in front of her and
issues a clear, low sound, less a growl than a warning a human might give.

When Black Heart is at the farthest point in his circle away from the house,
she again moves toward it. Again, he moves swiftly to block her. This time, his
warning is louder and more insistent. She backs up to her original spot. She
hears nothing but her voice against the inside of her ears and the swish of Black
Heart moving in the grass. *My God*, she thinks, *I'll have to sing all night.*

She wonders if she should run toward the house. She wonders if she should
shout Maria's name. But she fears—she knows—that if she broke off her song
even for a second, Black Heart would attack her, devour her.

As she sings, she prays Daniel will come home. She prays Ed and her
mother will become bored at the dinner and will drive the car into the middle
of the garden to save her. She prays Maria will step outside and Black Heart will
charge her, and this will give her the chance to flee. But the night radiates with
brilliant indifference and fatigue weighs on her like something living,
something growing. Her song has lost words.

*When they find me, they won't know he loved me. They'll think I was a
stupid girl who thought she could play with a mean dog.*

She feels her eyes flutter from fatigue; she feels herself stagger. As in a
dream, she feels Black Heart at her side, his head butting her thigh, insistent
and strong. He prods her toward the vineyard's open door. A moment later, she
is surrounded by grapes, silver-blue in the moonlight. Her **arid** mouth craves
their delicious juice, but Black Heart jabs her and she keeps moving. She hears
Maria calling her. She hears Ed's car limp up the gravel drive. She even hears,
or thinks she hears, Daniel, or perhaps it's her father, singing in the distance.

exhilaration:

arid:

107

260 The sounds fade. She wants to scream, but, so deep in the vineyard, she knows no one would hear her.

I'll find my way back, she vows, but stumbles, collapses. On her back on the grass altar, she sees, as if on a different planet, the snow-capped Andes. She discovers that, remarkably, she is still singing, in a voice charged with emotion. *I'm safe.* But—no—it is Black Heart, mouth at her ear, who is singing.

12. ◀ **REREAD** Reread lines 250–264. What do you think happens to Emily at the end of the story? Support your answer with explicit textual evidence.

_____

_____

_____

_____

SHORT RESPONSE

Cite Text Evidence   Identify the central theme of the story. What is the author saying about relationships? Review your reading notes, and be sure to **cite text evidence** in your response.

_____

_____

_____

_____

_____

_____

_____

_____

_____

_____

Background *Ever since the first farmers began to plant and harvest grains more than 10,000 years ago, humans have been looking for ways to increase agricultural production. Over the centuries and across the globe, farmers have developed tools and techniques to boost yields, such as irrigation, crop rotation, fertilizers and pesticides. Today's agricultural innovations are more effective than ever—but also more controversial.*

Are Genetically Modified Foods Scary?

Science Writing by Palome Reyes

CLOSE READ
Notes

1. **READ ▷** As you read lines 1–28, begin to collect and cite text evidence.

   • Underline the effects of the potato blight.
   • Circle the claim that is made about preventing "The Great Hunger."
   • Underline desired traits of genetically modified food in lines 18–28.

Ireland, between the years 1845 and 1852, experienced a seven-year siege of mass starvation, disease, and emigration known today as "The Great Hunger." During this time, approximately one million people starved to death and another two million fled for their lives, emigrating to England, America, Australia, New Zealand, Canada, and other countries. The immediate cause of the famine was a potato blight, a disease that ravaged potato crops throughout Europe. The impact was most severe in Ireland because one-third of the population was dependent on the potato crop for survival. Political, social, and economic factors only **exacerbated** the horrendous results of the potato blight

10 in Ireland.

exacerbated:

virulent:

Recent advances in the field of genetically modified (GM) food could have prevented the "Great Hunger" by introducing potatoes resistant to the disease that destroyed Ireland's potato crop. In the 1990s, Hawaii's papaya industry was facing disaster because of the **virulent** papaya ring spot virus. In this case, a genetically modified papaya *did* save the day. Developed and used since 1999, this genetically modified papaya, which resists the virus, has saved Hawaii's papaya industry.

The term "genetically modified food" refers to crop plants created for human and animal consumption that use the latest molecular biology 20 techniques to enhance desired traits, such as resistance to disease and herbicides or increased nutritional content. Traditionally this enhancement would have been done through plant breeding. But, breeding is time consuming and often not very accurate. Genetic engineering—actually isolating and inserting genes with the desirable trait into plants—can create plants with the desired trait very rapidly and with great accuracy. For example, plant geneticists can isolate a gene for pest resistance and insert that gene into another plant. The plant created as a result of the inserted genes will have the desired trait of being resistant to pests.

As exciting as the promise of GM foods may seem, some people are raising 30 questions about the safety and long-term effects of such foods. Although most

2. ◀ REREAD   Reread lines 18–28. Summarize the information in these lines to create a one-sentence definition of genetically modified food.

_____

_____

_____

_____

3. READ ▷   As you read lines 29–57, continue to cite textual evidence

- Underline text that explains doubts about GM food.
- Circle information that is presented as fact.
- In the margin, list one possible advantage of GM foods.

scientists **concur** that no harmful effects have yet been associated with consuming GM crops, the anti-GM-food people resist the idea of big agricultural and biotech companies (the forces spearheading production of GM foods) trying to control what goes into the food we eat. These opponents contend that genetic breeding is radically different from what human beings have previously done, and that, as a result, we are now consuming products that have never before been considered food. There is no way of predicting what long-term effects these plants may have on the human beings and animals that consume them. Neither is there any way of predicting what effect these

40 foods might have on other plants or on the environment in general. A widely publicized study published in the fall of 2012 only added fuel to the controversy when it noted that rats fed a lifetime diet of GM corn developed tumors, whereas those fed a non-GM diet did not.

Proponents of GM foods counter that GM plants, with their built-in protections against disease, pests, herbicides, cold, drought, and floods will help increase food production worldwide and thereby stem the tide of worldwide hunger. Furthermore, they argue that, although Americans have been eating GM food for years, no one has been able to cite a single case of someone actually getting sick from these foods.

concur:

50   It is difficult to ignore the fact that the majority of scientific research thus far indicates that GM foods pose no threat to consumers. On the other hand, eating is something that we all do every day. Should the choice about what we put into our mouths be left up to us or to businesses with financial interests in GM products? The GM opponents argue that the choice should be ours and that, at the very least, GM crops should be labeled. In this way consumers would know what they are eating and could, therefore, choose to take the risk or not.

4. ◀ REREAD AND DISCUSS   Reread lines 50–57. With a small group, discuss the idea of labeling GM food. Do you think this is a good option to please both GM opponents and supporters? Explain.

SHORT RESPONSE

Cite Text Evidence   Summarize the article in the lines below. First, identify the central idea and its most important details, and then retell them in your own words. Review your reading notes, and be sure to **cite text evidence** from the article in your response.

_____

_____

_____

_____

_____

_____

_____

_____

_____

Finding Ourselves in Nature

Finding Ourselves in Nature

"How often I've wanted to escape to a wilderness where a human hand has not been in everything."

—Linda Hogan

Background **Louise Erdrich** *is the author of thirteen novels, including* Love Medicine *and* The Round House, *which won the National Book Award for Fiction in 2012. Growing up, she was surrounded by a family of storytellers. Her mother was French Chippewa, her father was German American, and her grandfather was the tribal chairman at Turtle Mountain Reservation in North Dakota. An enrolled member of the Turtle Mountain Band of Chippewa Indians, Erdrich writes candidly about today's Native American societies and her own personal experiences as a mixed-heritage American.*

Local Deer

Essay by Louise Erdrich

CLOSE READ
Notes

1. **READD** ▶ As you read lines 1–19, begin to collect and cite text evidence.

   - Underline the active verbs used to describe the actions of the woodchuck pups.
   - Circle examples of figurative language used to describe the woodchucks or their actions.

The fat lady thins suddenly. A new company of woodchucks appears. There are five, and they tumble beneath my feet, knocking against the boards of the crawl space, chewing up the raisins and apples I leave by their hole. I begin to worry that the whole house may plunge into the earth. Week after week I watch the fat pups spill into the yard, tumbling onto one another, end over end, weaving themselves into a ball of woodchucks. They play under the house, sometimes right below my feet. No matter how hard I stomp they continue to loll and dig and play. They knock into the underground gas furnace, and love the big noise. I leave sliced apples outside the door. Cracked corn. Stale bread. I

10 spread the contents of a box of half-**petrified** prunes on the old wooden step. All of this they gobble down, running from below the house before I've even gone inside again. After a while they become tame as children and will approach my foot to take a peanut from the toe of my boot.

petrified:

115

So here I sit, with a peanut on my foot, as though I'm not a writer, as though I've got nothing to do but watch these careful nuisances steal toward me one muscle at a time. I should be working because our baby is asleep, but I am too busy training woodchucks. It is late summer now, the air filled with a round clarity. I'm thinking of a sentence, businesslike, a thing I can write down, when I look up from my woodchuck.

20   A young buck deer is watching me.

I've never seen one here before, although they leave their tracks, two split moons, at the edge of the field and far from the road. I've fixed No Hunting signs into the sides of the trees. I've watched. I've waited the way my father taught me to wait for deer. But New Hampshire's deer herd is about half the size of Vermont's and they are nowhere near the nuisance they are in the northeastern suburbs. Simple politics. I live in a section of the state where for the price of a license a hunter can shoot any deer, doe, or fawn. Vermont has more restrictive laws, it also has a bigger winter kill-off. Deer eat rare plants as well as boring shrubs, so I know they're a mixed blessing. It is our human fault

30   that they're now pests in many areas. At any rate, the deer I see are an unusual presence in my hunted-down stretch of the Northeast.

2. **◀ REREAD** As you reread lines 1–13, list in the margin the different images the descriptions of the woodchucks bring to mind. How does the author use figurative language to present a detailed picture of these animals? Support your answer with explicit textual evidence.

_____

_____

_____

_____

3. **READ ▶** As you read lines 20–57, continue to cite textual evidence.

• Underline all the references to looking, seeing, watching, visibility, and invisibility.

• Circle short sentences that interrupt the author's descriptions.

• In the margin, make notes about the attitude and behavior of the young buck.

"He is the bronze of dead pine needles and his eyes are black rimmed in black, still and large."

The young buck stands fifteen feet away, under the old apple tree someone planted here a hundred years ago. His antlers are small, still cased in velvet.[1] He is the bronze of dead pine needles and his eyes are black rimmed in black, still and large. His neck is limber and strong. When a car passes, he freezes, but he does not move. I don't move either. He watches me carefully and then with nervous care he reaches down and picks up a hard, green apple. His head jerks up and he looks straight at me, the apple round and whole in his teeth, like the apple in the mouth of a suckling pig.

40   The apple begins to vanish. His tongue extends and pushes the whole thing back into his throat. I am alarmed, suddenly, as when one of my children bites off a piece of something too large to swallow. I mentally review the Heimlich maneuver.[2] But the apple vanishes. He reaches down for another. And then, through the wide screen door, he hears the baby shake her rattle. She has awakened and she **brandishes** her toy at the buck. He takes one step backward, and stands in an attitude of absolute alertness, testing the noise. The rattle spins again. He turns. He walks carefully into the trees.

    Deer return until the apples are gone, a doe with the young buck. She is the same shade of russet,[3] her wide-set ears flickering and nervous, all air and
50   grace. I look up and she is watching me, her eyes deep-water mussels, endless and grave, purple-black. She moves from the brush. Her tail is long, a dog's tail, curved and sinuous, tipped with black. She sweeps it back and forth as she browses. I grow used to them and soon I find that the deer are there, always

brandishes:

---

[1] **velvet:** a soft, fuzzy layer of skin that covers a male deer's antlers while they are growing.
[2] **Heimlich maneuver:** first aid technique to dislodge an obstruction from the throat of a person who is choking.
[3] **russet:** reddish brown in color.

there, in the shadows and the shapes of other things. Invisible and obvious, gray as talc and calm as sand, the deer divide themselves from the spars[4] and bones of trees. They make themselves whole suddenly. I am not looking, and then I am looking into their eyes.

---

[4] **spars:** thick, strong poles, such as those used for a mast in a ship.

4. **◀ REREAD** As you reread 48–57, note the author's description of the doe. How does her word choice affect your vision of the animal?

_____

_____

_____

SHORT RESPONSE

Cite Text Evidence In what way does the author's style help you understand her attitude towards the animals in her yard? Analyze Erdrich's style, including her use of figurative language. Review your reading notes, and be sure to **cite text evidence** in your response.

_____

_____

_____

_____

_____

_____

_____

_____

_____

_____

Background *Pastoral poetry—a tradition stretching back to the ancient Greeks—presents an idealized vision of simple country life, describing bucolic landscapes, shepherds and their flocks, and the glory of nature. Even after its popularity faded in the eighteenth century, poets continued to refer to the pastoral style and ideas—contrasting rural and urban settings, and lamenting the loss of a simpler and truer connection between humankind and the natural world.*

Pastorals

William Carlos Williams *(1883–1963), one of the most influential poets of the twentieth century, lived most of his life in Rutherford, New Jersey. He was both a doctor and a writer, keeping up a medical practice and becoming a prolific and successful poet, playwright, essayist, and novelist. Williams advocated "the local," taking his subject matter from the lives and circumstances of ordinary people. "Pastoral" is one of several poems he wrote with the same name.*

Jennifer Chang *was also born in New Jersey. "Pastoral" is from her first book of poems,* The History of Anonymity, *published in 2008. Her poetry has appeared in many prestigious publications, including* Poetry, The New Republic, The Kenyon Review, *and* The Nation. *Her lyrical poems often connect the natural world with the emotional world of the self. Chang also co-chairs the advisory board of Kundiman, an organization dedicated to the support and promotion of Asian American poetry.*

1. **READ** ▶ As you read "Pastoral" by William Carlos Williams,
    begin to collect and cite text evidence.

    • Underline words and phrases that contrast with nature.

    • In the margin, explain the contrast.

Pastoral

William Carlos Williams

The little sparrows
hop ingenuously
about the pavement
quarreling
5   with sharp voices
over those things
that interest them.
But we who are wiser
shut ourselves in
10   on either hand
and no one knows
whether we think good
or evil.

                Meanwhile,
15   the old man who goes about
gathering dog-lime
walks in the gutter
without looking up
and his tread
20   is more majestic than
that of the Episcopal minister
approaching the pulpit
of a Sunday.
                These things
25   astonish me beyond words.

2. **◀ REREAD**   Reread the poem. How do the final two lines affect your
    understanding of the poem?

_____

_____

3. **READ ▶** As you read "Pastoral" by Jennifer Chang, continue to cite text evidence.

- Circle each use of the word *something*.
- Underline text that describes something wrong or unnatural.
- In the margin, note when the speaker seems uncertain.

Pastoral
Jennifer Chang

Something in the field is
working away. Root-noise.
Twig-noise. Plant
of weak chlorophyll, no
5   name for it. Something
in the field has mastered
distance by living too close
to fences. Yellow fruit, has it
pit or seeds? Stalk of wither. Grass-
10 noise fighting weed-noise. Dirt
and chant. Something in the
field. Coreopsis.¹ I did not mean
to say that. Yellow petal, has it
wither-gift? Has it gorgeous
15 rash? Leaf-loss and worried
sprout, its bursting art. Something in the. Field fallowed and
cicada. I did not mean to
say. Has it roar and bloom?
20 Has it road and follow? A thistle
prick, fraught burrs, such
easy attachment. Stem-
and stamen-noise. Can I lime-
flower? Can I chamomile?²
25 Something in the field cannot.

---

¹ **coreopsis:** a plant of the daisy family, with bright yellow flowers.
² **chamomile:** an herb also of the daisy family, with small, aromatic white flowers often used to make an herbal tea.

4. **◄ REREAD** As you reread the poem, note the poet's use of sentence fragments, hyphenated words, non-traditional syntax, and sudden line breaks. How does this chaotic structure affect your experience as a reader?

_____

_____

_____

_____

_____

SHORT RESPONSE

Cite Text Evidence Compare how the two poems entitled "Pastoral"—published almost 100 years apart—play on the traditional pastoral form, which presents idealized scenes of nature. What is each poem saying about the relationship between humankind and nature? Be sure to **cite text evidence** in your response.

_____

_____

_____

_____

_____

_____

_____

_____

_____

_____

Background **Baron Wormser** *is a widely-acclaimed American poet born in Baltimore, Maryland, in 1948. From 1975 to 1998, he lived "off the grid" with his wife and children on 48 acres of pristine woodland in Mercer, Maine, earning a living as a librarian and creative writing teacher. He wrote a book about the experience called* The Road Washes Out in Spring *from which this excerpt is taken. In 2000, he was appointed Poet Laureate of Maine. Since 2002, Wormser has been conducting poetry writing workshops with students and teachers in schools and universities throughout Maine.*

Trees

Essay by Baron Wormser

CLOSE READ
Notes

1. **READ** ▷ As you read lines 1–20, begin to cite textual evidence.

   • Underline text describing what the author did to build his dream house.
   • Circle text describing the results of these actions.
   • In the margin, make notes about what the author values (lines 12–20).

Our house was quite literally in the woods. I cut down poplars, a few spavined[1] apple trees, some white pines, and a number of tall, thin, red maples to create an adequate opening to situate the house and let the sun in over the tree tops. The apple trees must have been the remnant of a little orchard that had been planted near where the farmhouse once stood. The others had grown up randomly as the site of what once was a farm became woods. We used a compass to **orient** the house to the south. This was not a development lot that had to have its house squarely facing the street. The sun that came up over the trees could be seen from our bedroom window. We could follow it across the front of the house throughout the day. On a frigid but sunny winter day, the south windows **suffused** a gentle warmth.

orient:

suffuse:

10

---

[1] **spavined:** damaged, deteriorated, or ruined.

In front of and in back of the house stood a number of very straight pines that were fifty to sixty years old. We revered them, though we knew any city person strolling in a park—a domain where aesthetics trumped board feet— would see larger and older trees. In rural Maine lumbering is always an issue; one sees very few, really old trees in the endless woods because those woods are being cut time and time again. The works of man, the industry that drives each economic day, are what the Maine woods call to mind. What man leaves behind is happenstance. The cutters might trust **indomitable** nature; they
20 might trust cooperative, university-based science; or they might be indifferent.

When I first began to roam the backcountry where we lived, I was routinely appalled when I encountered tracts that had been lumbered recently. Limbs and sections of trunks that were unusable were strewn everywhere. Young trees had been toppled and left eventually to collapse under snow. Splintered trees whose tops had been sheared off when other trees fell on them stood like big, ragged toothpicks. Huge ruts from the skidders that moved the logs were everywhere. Piles of brush sat like so much unwanted debris. It looked like a war had occurred, a war against the trees. Of course, woodcutting isn't an issue of beautification. It's an issue of humankind making a buck off
30 some trees that the rest of humankind needs for paper and lumber. The whole notion of trees as something to regard and **venerate** would have seemed bizarre to the men with the chainsaws and trucks. The trees were there for people to use. Such is the way of workaday humanity.

indomitable:

venerate:

2. **◄ REREAD** Reread lines 12–20. Make an inference about the author's feelings about lumbering. Cite evidence from the text.

_____

_____

_____

_____

3. **READ ▶** As you read lines 21–51, continue to cite textual evidence.

- Circle text that describes the author's initial reaction toward lumbering.
- Underline details that explain why trees are cut down.
- In the margin, note how the author describes recently lumbered tracts (lines 23–28).

CLOSE READ
Notes

We were fortunate. For us, the trees were not part of any crucial, economic equation. When I cut trees for the firewood that kept us warm and that heated our water, I could pick each tree I was going to fell according to how healthy (or unhealthy) the tree was and whether I should thin that one to allow others to grow. I could fell the tree so it would do the least damage to others. I could use virtually the entire tree because I sawed up the limbs for our cook stove. I could
40   arrange the brush on the ground so that it would compact reasonably quickly. You had to take a careful look to notice that a tree had been felled.

    Although we heated our house with the trees I cut on our land and although we had no backup heat whatsoever, more than one woodcutter told me that, despite my exertions, I was doing little more in the woods than playing. I could understand. Anything that didn't honor the dollar equation was recreation. Caleb cut trees, sold them for pulp, and used the money to pay for oil heat. He informed me he was "way ahead" by doing this. When I asked him, "Ahead of what?" he only snorted. He had endured a lifetime of starting fires in wood stoves, getting up in the middle of winter nights to put in more
50   wood, then waking in the morning to the cold misery of ashes. I could have it. I was off in my labor-intensive poetic Oz.

    I had to confess that I was quite happy in my Oz of trees. At any time I could walk a few steps and literally be in the woods. In the heat of summer, I had the shade, the coolness, and the ever-changing play of the sifted light. The

---

4. **◀ REREAD** Reread lines 42–51. What does Caleb mean when he says he "was way ahead?" Support your answer with explicit textual evidence.

_____

_____

_____

---

5. **READ ▶** As you read lines 52–90, continue to cite textual evidence.

- Underline text the author uses instead of "trees."
- Circle the sensory language the author uses to describe the trees.

CLOSE READ
Notes

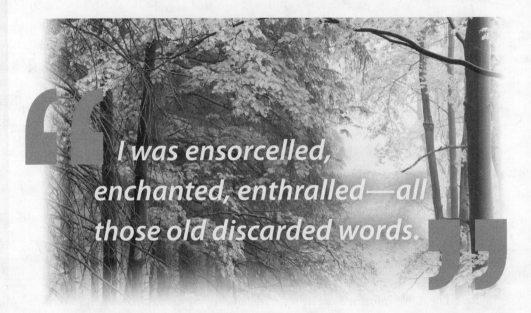

I was ensorcelled, enchanted, enthralled—all those old discarded words.

protuberant:

analogies to a cathedral were not far-fetched. In the heights of the trees there was audible mystery—pewees and tanagers[2] I heard but rarely saw. I marveled at the relentless yearning toward the sun, how the maples made their way amid a canopy of pines. In winter I watched the bare forms gesturing like still dancers. I listened to the spry clatter of branches in a strong wind. They

60   sounded like little bones. In all seasons, the waver and dapple of shadow sighed. When I examined a stump, I saw in the growth rings the shapes of years, some bunched, some even, some **protuberant**. I was ensorcelled, enchanted, enthralled—all those old discarded words.

Part of living with the trees lay in considering their ways. Each type of tree was deeply singular. There were the trademark white pines that a friend once likened to huge stalks of celery on account of how their tops waved in a wind. There were the smooth-trunked beeches that held onto their parchment-like leaves throughout the winter and rattled dryly. There were the poplars (or "popple" in the local designation) that were "trash" trees, their loosely fibrous

70   wood considered not good for much of anything. Their diminutive leaves were attuned to every breeze and shimmered with audible movement. In a stiff wind they seemed almost frenetic. There were the deeply furrowed sugar maples along the road to our house that had been tapped to make maple syrup and now were dying as their huge limbs rotted and fell. There were the white birches, with their peeling, papery strips of bark, yellow birches that were not a bright yellow, but a silvery yellow, and gray birches that sometimes were bent almost to the ground from the winter's snow.

And there were the elms left over from the nineteenth century when farmers had planted whips—slender, unbranched shoots of American elm—to

80   domesticate and beautify the homestead. It was sad to see them—massive

---

[2] **pewees and tanagers:** two types of perching birds.

126

torsos that the seasons were breaking down bit by bit. The wood was gnarled and almost impossible to split. Occasionally, we came upon them in the middle of what seemed like nowhere but wasn't—once a farmhouse had stood there. Sentinels, the elms had died on their watch. Nearby, weathered clapboards soft with decay lay on the ground along with the usual array of rusty pots, pans, and broken crockery. We stared up at the dead trees and down at the shards of lives. The massive, leafless stillness spoke to the wretched indifference of time. Their ruined dignity warned the **encroaching** woods that the arboreal world was a mere wink. Even the most stolid matter was corruptible. They were
90   sculptures of loss.

     When I looked at one of my familiars, such as the pine in back of our house that had grown up in a gigantic U-shape, two fifty-foot limbs rising from the trunk at around thirty feet, I considered the hazards of growth. Some impediment had caused this curious formation. The awkward tree kept growing as I kept on living. Habit had a sort of genius, yet it might take shapes that made the eye wince. I thought of the terrible ability of living creatures to adapt, to get along, to say the current regime is okay when the current regime is not okay. Eventually a windstorm would wreck those two unnatural limbs that had become trunks. The tree would have lived a reasonably long life, however.
100   Like many people under many regimes, it had managed. Its awkwardness had not been ruinous; its inconvenience was silent.

     The bark was surprisingly delicate, and the pitch was sticky. The fragrance was that thick, turpentine sweetness that is pine. I didn't have a problem understanding how people had once worshipped trees. Perhaps, as pantheists[3]

encroaching:

---

[3] **pantheists:** people who believe that God is identical with the universe.

---

6. **◀ REREAD** Reread lines 78–90. Make an inference about what the author means when he describes the trees as "sculptures of loss?"

_____

_____

_____

---

7. **READ ▶** As you read lines 91–108, continue to cite textual evidence.

- Underline details that describe the unusual pine in the back of the house.
- In the margin, explain what the trees teach the author about adaptation.

felt, God spoke through the trees. It seemed a pretty thought but an unnecessary one. I wasn't inclined to look further or deeper than what I saw and smelled and heard. If my senses were stupid and childlike, so be it. These great, leafy delusions were vulnerable, yet **stalwart**.

stalwart:

8. **◀ REREAD** Reread lines 91–101. Why does the author call the ability to adapt "terrible"? Cite evidence from the text.

_____

_____

_____

SHORT RESPONSE

Cite Text Evidence   In what way has Wormser's view of the natural world changed over the years? Make inferences about the author's point of view, **citing text evidence** in your response.

_____

_____

_____

_____

_____

_____

_____

_____

_____

_____

_____

Acknowledgments

Excerpts from *Beowulf,* translated by Burton Raffel. Text copyright © 1963, renewed © 1991 by Burton Raffel. Reprinted by permission of Dutton Signet, a division of Penguin Group (USA) Inc. and Russell & Volkening as agents for the author.

"Blackheart" by Mark Brazaitis from *Witness*, Vol. XXV No. 2. Text copyright © Summer 2012 by Mark Brazaitis. Reprinted by permission of Black Mountain Institute at University of Nevada, Las Vegas.

Excerpts from *The Canterbury Tales* by Geoffrey Chaucer, translated by Nevill Coghill. Text copyright © 1951 by Nevill Coghill. Reprinted by permission of Curtis Brown Group Ltd. on behalf of the Estate of Nevill Coghill.

"Elsewhere" from *The Arkansas Testament* by Derek Walcott. Text copyright © 1987 by Derek Walcott. Reprinted by permission of Farrar Straus and Giroux LLC and Faber and Faber Ltd.

Excerpt from "Interview with Bill Moyers" by Martín Espada. Text copyright © by Martín Espada. Reprinted by permission of Martín Espada.

Kewauna's Ambition" (retitled excerpt from *How Children Succeed: Grit, Curiosity, and the Hidden Power of Character*) by Paul Tough. Text copyright © 2012 by Paul Tough. Reprinted by permission of Houghton Mifflin Publishing Company, Random House Group Ltd., Tantor Media and the Abner Stein Agency.

"Local Deer" from *The Blue Jay's Dance: A Birth Year* by Louise Erdrich. Text copyright © 1995 by Louise Erdrich. Reprinted by permission of HarperCollins Publishers.

"Next Term, We'll Mash You" from *Pack of Cards and Other Stories* by Penelope Lively. Text copyright © 1978 by Penelope Lively. Reprinted by permission of Grove Atlantic, Inc., the Emma Sweeney Agency on behalf of the author, and David Higham and Associates Ltd.

"Nobel Peace Prize Lecture" (retitled from "Nobel Lecture") by Wangari Maathai. Text copyright © 2004 by The Nobel Foundation. Reprinted by permission of The Nobel Foundation.

Excerpt from on-stage conversation with Robert Finch, Utah Museum of Natural History, October 1987. Text copyright © 1987 by Terry Tempest Williams. Reprinted by permission of Terry Tempest Williams.

"Pastoral" from *The Collected Poems of William Carlos Williams, Vol. I* by William Carlos Williams. Text copyright © 1986 by New Directions Publishing Corporation. Reprinted by permission of New Directions Publishing Corporation and Carcanet Press.

"Pastoral" from *The History of Anonymity* by Jennifer Chang. Text copyright © 2008 by University of Georgia Press. Reprinted by permission of University of Georgia Press.

"Pink Think" (retitled excerpt from *Pink Think: Becoming a Woman in Many Uneasy Lessons*) by Lynn Peril. Text copyright © 2002 by Lynn Peril. Reprinted by permission of W.W. Norton & Company, Inc.

"A Right to Choose a Single Sex Education" by Kay Bailey Hutchison and Barbara Mikulski from *The Wall Street Journal*, October 16, 2012, *online.wsj.com*. Text copyright © 2012 by Kay Bailey Hutchison. Reprinted by permission of former U.S. Senator Kay Bailey Hutchison.

"Trees" (retitled excerpt from *The Road Washes Out in Spring*) by Baron Wormser. Text copyright © 2006 by Baron Wormser. Reprinted by permission of University Press of New England.

"Who Speaks for the 1%," by Joel Stein from *Time* Magazine, October 31, 2011, www.timemagazine.com. Text copyright © 2011 by Time, Inc. Reprinted by permission of Time, Inc.

Index of Titles & Authors